NAPOLEON'S INVASION OF
RUSSIA

SPECIAL CAMPAIGN SERIES.　　No. 19

NAPOLEON'S INVASION OF RUSSIA

By

Lieut.-Colonel R. G. BURTON

Indian Army

AUTHOR OF "NAPOLEON'S CAMPAIGNS IN ITALY,"
"FROM BOULOGNE TO AUSTERLITZ," ETC.

WITH SIX MAPS AND PLANS

"Les grandes entreprises lointaines périssent par la grandeur même des préparatifs qu'on fait pour en assurer la réussite."

MONTESQUIEU.

The Naval & Military Press Ltd

Published by

The Naval & Military Press Ltd
Unit 5 Riverside, Brambleside
Bellbrook Industrial Estate
Uckfield, East Sussex
TN22 1QQ England

Tel: +44 (0)1825 749494

www.naval-military-press.com
www.nmarchive.com

Cover illustration:
The French Army crossing the Berezina by January Suchodolski

In reprinting in facsimile from the original, any imperfections are inevitably reproduced and the quality may fall short of modern type and cartographic standards.

Print and page size has been increased over the original publications to accommodate the oversized maps.

PREFACE

WHILE the great tragedy of 1812 must ever excite the interest and wonder of mankind, like all the deeds of its mighty actor, the lessons to be derived from it are its most important if not its most attractive feature. We may point to the vanity of human greatness, here shown in its decline, and the limitations imposed by adverse circumstance on genius even in its most exalted manifestation. We may indicate the futility of undertaking a great enterprise with inadequate means, without the power and perhaps even the will to carry it to a successful conclusion; and the limits that are fixed to human ambition as much by the forces of nature as by the hostility of man. Napoleon, the embodiment of intellectual force, the incarnation of mental and physical energy, contrived for a time to control the conditions he created in Europe. He rode the whirlwind by virtue of character, of personality, of intelligence, and of imagination which made up the sum of his genius. But in course of time he created forces, not only in his enemies but in himself, which ranged beyond the power of control. There arose in him an almost blasphemous self-confidence a belief in his " star " that led him to neglect the elements necessary to success, which may be illustrated by his own saying: "It is a proof of the weakness of human nature that men imagine that they can oppose me." Well might Goethe say of him: "He lives entirely in the ideal but can never consciously grasp it."

The military lessons of the Russian campaign are numerous. In its general features, in the grandeur of its conception, and in some respects in its execution, as well as in its abysmal end, this gigantic invasion was splendid and awe-inspiring. Who can contemplate unmoved the sublime spectacle of that mighty human stream pouring across Europe into Russia, fighting its way to Moscow, and its shattered remnants struggling back across the Berezina, in whose icy flood so many thousand lives were quenched in circumstances of tragic horror. The dramatic figure of the Great Emperor, standing in the snow during the retreat, dominating the situation by the mere terror of his personality, will stand out for ever on the page of history. The fortitude in the retreat of Ney, that warrior of transcendent courage, who, asked where was the rearguard, replied in all truth, "I am the rearguard"; and in response to a summons to surrender, "A Marshal of France never surrenders!" furnishes one of the finest episodes of this dramatic epoch.

As regards the fundamental causes of failure, speculation leads us to inquire into the personal attributes of the greatest soldier of all history. There appears to be no doubt that at this time, although Napoleon's intellect retained all its sharpness and his vision all its clearness, his physical nature had begun to decline. Already in his forty-third year he had lost in physical and mental vigour, and in decision and boldness of execution. The first failure of his plans—the escape of Bagration—would have been averted had Napoleon been the general of 1805. But he contented himself with sitting in his study at Vilna, and issuing orders which were sound in project but faulty in execution. Nor do we find him dominating the battlefield at Borodino as he did at Rivoli, at Austerlitz, and at Jena.

But in spite of failure, when all has been considered, the campaign of 1812 will remain for all time one of the most wonderful episodes in the history of the world, sufficient of itself to secure eternal fame to the Man of whom it has been said by Napier:

" To have struggled with hope under such astounding difficulties was scarcely to be expected from the greatest minds. But like the emperor to calculate and combine the most stupendous efforts with calmness and accuracy; to seize every favourable chance with unerring rapidity; to sustain every reverse with undisturbed constancy, never urged to rashness by despair yet enterprising to the utmost verge of daring consistent with reason, was a display of intellectual greatness so surpassing, that it is not without justice Napoleon has been called, in reference as well to past ages as to the present, the foremost of mankind."

The author is greatly indebted to General Bogdanovich's history of the war, published in St Petersburg in 1859. The accuracy of Bogdanovich's narrative has been tested by reference to the correspondence of Napoleon.

Among other works to which reference has been made may be mentioned those of De Segur, Marbot, Labaume, Chambray, Fezensac, Jomini, Buturlin and Mikhailovski-Danilevski. The author has also had the advantage of traversing the route taken by the Grand Army in the advance to Moscow.

TABLE OF CONTENTS

CHAPTER I

THE CAUSES OF WAR

PAGE

Maritime Equilibrium—The Ambition of Napoleon—Sea Power—The Berlin Decree—Napoleon and Poland — Policy of Annexation — Controversy with Russia 1

CHAPTER II

PREPARATIONS FOR WAR

Napoleon's Preparations—Formation of the Grand Army — Davout's Corps — Organisation of Armies — Supplies — Transport — Bridging Materials—Further Organisation—Intelligence—Preparations of the Tzar—Russian Plans—Napoleon's Plan—Napoleon at Dresden . 7

CHAPTER III

THE OPPOSING FORCES

The Grand Army — Character of the Army — Davout's Corps — The French Leaders — The Russian Armies — Character of the Russian Army — System of Enlistment — Martial Qualities — Russian Cavalry — Artillery — The Cossacks—Russian Officers—Staff—Administration — Russian Commanders — Positions of Opposing Armies 17

CONTENTS

CHAPTER IV

THE THEATRE OF WAR . . . 41

CHAPTER V

THE INVASION OF LITHUANIA

General Distribution—Russians—French—Napoleon on the Niemen—Forward Movement—Passage of the River—Napoleon's Plan—Further Advance The Russians surprised—General Russian Retreat—French Advance—Napoleon's Dispositions—Movements of the King of Westphalia—Bagration's Retreat—Pursuit of Bagration—Weather Conditions—Difficulties of Supply and Transport—Comments . . . 48

CHAPTER VI

THE ADVANCE TO THE DWINA

Napoleon's Plan—The Russians at Drissa—Oudinot's Advance—Macdonald's Movements—Napoleon leaves Vilna—The Movement towards Vitebsk—Action at Ostrovno—Napoleon at Ostrovno—Operations at Vitebsk—Forward Movement—Operations against Bagration—Oudinot and Wittgenstein—Movements of Schwarzenberg—Comments 63

CHAPTER VII

FROM THE DWINA TO THE DNIEPER

Napoleon at Vitebsk—Distribution of the French Forces—Russians assume the Offensive—Skirmish at Inkovo—French Dispositions—Russian Movements—Napoleon's Advance—Passage of the Dnieper—Cavalry Action at Krasnoi—Russian Dispositions—Comments . . 80

CHAPTER VIII

THE BATTLE OF SMOLENSK

Smolensk—Raevski's defensive Measures—Napoleon arrives before Smolensk—French Dispositions—Russian Plans—Bagration's Retreat—Attack on Smolensk — Russian Retirement — Napoleon enters Smolensk—Barclay's Retreat continued—Action at Lubino—Comments—The Decision to advance on Moscow 91

CHAPTER IX

THE ADVANCE TO BORODINO

Russian Desire for Battle — French Pursuit — Napoleon leaves Smolensk—Measures in Rear—Russian Retreat continued—Kutuzov assumes Command—Action at Shivardino—Position of Borodino—Occupation of the Position—The Opposing Forces — French Dispositions—Napoleon's Orders 108

CHAPTER X

THE BATTLE OF BORODINO

Napoleon at Shivardino—Attack on the Russian Left—Eugene takes Borodino—Renewed Attack on Russian Left—Ney assaults the Left—Russians retake the Redoubts—Poniatovski's Advance—The Battle at Semyonovskaya—French capture the Left Redoubts—Murat's Cavalry Charge—Capture of Semyonovskaya—Poniatovski at Utitza—The Battle in the Centre—Reinforcement of the Russian Left—Uvarov's Cavalry Charge—Renewed Attack on the Centre—Capture of Raevski's Battery—The Battle ends—Russian Position—Comments . . 124

CHAPTER XI

The Occupation of Moscow

Russian Retreat—The Russians abandon Moscow—Napoleon enters Moscow—The Burning of the City—Russian March to Podolsk—Pursuit by French Advanced Guard—French Movements—Napoleon proposes Peace—Measures for the Future—Napoleon's Appreciation of the Situation—The Question of Retreat—Action at Vinkovo—Evacuation of Moscow—Operations on the Dwina—Events in Volhynia . . 143

CHAPTER XII

From Moscow to Maloyaroslavetz

March of the Grand Army—Kutuzov leaves Tarutino — Maloyaroslavetz — Advance or Retreat ? — Retreat—Comments 169

CHAPTER XIII

The Retreat to Smolensk

The March to Vyazma—Russian Movements—Napoleon at Vyazma—News from the Wings—Napoleon's Measures — Retreat continued — Kutuzov's Pursuit—Battle of Vyazma—Difficulties of the March—Kutuzov's Plans—Retreat to Smolensk—Ney's Rearguard—The Passage of the Vop—Russian Operations . . . 177

CHAPTER XIV

From Smolensk to Borisov

Retreat from Smolensk—Arrival at Krasnoi—Napoleon's Resolution—Battle of Krasnoi—Ney's Rearguard — From Krasnoi to Borisov—Action at Borisov—Chichagov's Movements—Disposition of Opposing Forces . . 192

CHAPTER XV

THE PASSAGE OF THE BEREZINA

The Point of Passage—Construction of Bridges—26th November—27th November—Capture of a French Division—Passage continued—Battle of the Berezina—Repulse of Russians on both Banks—Comments—Napoleon on the Berezina   205

CHAPTER XVI

FROM THE BEREZINA TO THE NIEMEN

Retreat from the Berezina—Napoleon leaves the Army—The Army reaches Vilna—Passage of the Niemen—Ney's Last Stand—Macdonald's Retreat—Schwarzenberg's Retirement .   .   219

CHAPTER XVII

THE CAUSES OF FAILURE   225

MAPS AND PLANS

1. Map of the Theatre of Operations.
2. Map to illustrate the Operations round Smolensk.
3. Plan of Smolensk and its Environs.
4. The Battle of Borodino.
5. From Moscow to Smolensk.
6. The Passage of the Berezina.

NAPOLEON'S INVASION OF RUSSIA

CHAPTER I

THE CAUSES OF WAR

Maritime Equilibrium—The Ambition of Napoleon—Sea Power—The Berlin Decree—Napoleon and Poland—Policy of Annexation—Controversy with Russia

Maritime Equilibrium

MARITIME equilibrium is no less a part of the balance of power than Continental equilibrium. This truth, recognised by Napoleon, but ignored by other Powers on the Continent during the struggles of the Napoleonic epoch, was at the base of the causes which led up to the invasion of Russia; it was the fundamental reason of the prolonged contest between England and France; and it is the prime factor in world-politics to-day.

Thus, although Napoleon had made himself master in continental Europe, his power was insecure so long as English ships could sail the seas unchallenged, and stand between him and the dominion of the world. And war with Russia arose in the first instance from the establishment of his "continental system," by which he hoped to destroy the maritime supremacy of England.

While this and other factors contributed to annul the Peace of Tilsit, the immediate cause of hostilities lay in the ambition of the Man whose war eagles were carried from Madrid to Moscow, and who occupied in turn the most important capitals of Europe. In all probability he looked beyond Russia into Asia, for even after his expedition to Egypt the glamour of the East had always attracted him, since the days when he said : "My glory is already at an end ; there is not enough of it in this little Europe. I must go to the East ; all great glory comes from there." This predilection for Oriental conquest cropped up continually throughout his career. It was the motive of his treaty with the Shah of Persia in 1807. It was discussed at Tilsit with the Tzar Alexander in 1808. An expedition to Egypt was to sail from Corfu, while the united armies of Russia, France and Austria were to march on India. In the same year he instructed his librarian to " collect memoirs about the campaigns which have taken place on the Euphrates and against the Parthians, beginning with that of Crassus down to the eighth century . . . to mark on maps the route which each army followed." Again in 1811 we find him considering expeditions against Egypt and Ireland. If these succeeded, he would extend his

Empire far to the East and West. "They wish to know where we are going, where I shall plant the new 'Pillars of Hercules.' We will make an end of Europe, and then as robbers throw themselves on others less bold, we will cast ourselves on India, which the latter class have mastered." "Three years more," he exclaimed to the Bavarian Minister, "and I am Lord of the Universe." So it is quite probable that he looked on his expedition to Russia as a prelude to conquests farther East. Nor can we say that Jomini was without reason in accusing the English of "declaiming ceaselessly against the insatiable ambition of the French Government, while obtaining possession without plausible motive of an empire of a hundred million human beings in Asia."

While Austerlitz, Jena and Tilsit made Napoleon supreme on the continent of Europe, the battle of Trafalgar gave England maritime supremacy throughout the world. If the balance of power was upset in Europe, it was no less destroyed on the sea, where England was rendered immune from the attacks of the conqueror. Seeing the hopelessness of reducing England by force of arms, Napoleon attempted to wreck her commerce by a decree. The English Government had issued an Order in Council declaring the coast of France from Anvers to Havre to be in a state of blockade.

Sea Power

Napoleon, in retaliation, by the famous decree of

Berlin of 21st November 1806, instituted his "continental system," according to which not only was England de-

The Berlin Decree clared in a state of blockade, but all commerce and all relations with Great Britain were forbidden in countries occupied by the French armies and their allies, and all merchandise and manufactures of Great Britain and her colonies were declared confiscated. In addition, all Continental ports were to be closed to English shipping.

Russia, detached from England at the Treaty of Tilsit, which followed on the Friedland Campaign, became a subscriber to this system, while the Tzar succumbed to the genius and the personality of Napoleon.

In the rearrangement of Europe which followed on the Jena Campaign and the meeting at Tilsit, the Grand

Napoleon and Poland Duchy of Warsaw was created out of the Polish provinces torn from Prussia. To set up a kingdom of Poland would be an offence to the Tzar, and Napoleon agreed that he would never establish such a kingdom, and would not further enlarge the duchy. Having settled with Russia, he turned to Spain and Portugal, from which his attention was again diverted by fresh hostilities with Austria. There followed the Peace of Vienna after the events of Ratisbon, Aspern and Wagram. One of the clauses of the new treaty provided for the cession of half of Galicia to the Duchy of Warsaw, which was thus elevated into the dimensions of a small kingdom. This measure, in direct contravention to the engagements made at Tilsit, alarmed the Tzar of Russia, who remonstrated in vain with Caulaincourt, the French Ambassador.

It was now clear that Napoleon aspired to universal Empire. He espoused the daughter of the Austrian Emperor, after a union with the Russian Grand Duchess Anne had been considered. In the same year, 1810, he issued decrees annexing Rome, Holland, and the German coast to Hamburg and Lubeck on the Baltic, which involved the expulsion of the Duke of Oldenburg, brother-in-law of the Tzar, whose dignity was thus further offended.

Policy of Annexation

A long diplomatic correspondence followed, accompanied by mutual complaints and recriminations. The Tzar complained of the aggrandisement of the Duchy of Warsaw in contravention of the Articles of Tilsit, the treatment of the Duke of Oldenburg and the annexation of North Germany to the French Empire. Napoleon taxed him in return with failure to observe the Continental system. But these negotiations only prolonged the period of preparation for war. While the Tzar cannot be exonerated from all blame for the rupture of peace, it was manifest that Napoleon desired war. He could count on the support of Austria. He proposed, in order to gain over the Poles, to re-establish the kingdom of Poland at the expense of Russia, who had

Controversy with Russia

absorbed the greater part of her territory. He was in a position to coerce Prussia. He hoped to obtain the co-operation or at least the neutrality of Sweden, which was ruled by Bernadotte, a former marshal of France, and thus secure the left flank of his advance; while on the right Russia was engaged on the Danube in war with Turkey, the continuance of which might be ensured by wise diplomacy.

CHAPTER II

PREPARATIONS FOR WAR

Napoleon's Preparations—Formation of the Grand Army—Davout's Corps — Organisation of Armies — Supplies — Transport — Bridging Materials — Further Organisation —Intelligence—Preparations of the Tzar—Russian Plans—Napoleon's Plan—Napoleon at Dresden

NAPOLEON'S preparations for war with Russia began with the calling out for service in December 1810 of the conscripts of 1811, to the number of 80,000 men. The Emperor next undertook the fortification of Dantzig and the strengthening of its garrison. At the end of June 1811 Davout's corps of observation on the Elbe, having headquarters at Hamburg, was strengthened to over 51,000 men; in July the cavalry was reorganised and a regiment of Polish lancers was raised at Warsaw. By August Davout had 70,000 men; the Saxon corps, 22,000; and the troops of the Grand Duchy of Warsaw numbered 60,000. In October the number of French troops in Northern Germany, together with the garrisons of the fortresses on the Oder, reached nearly 90,000 men. There were in addition 24,000 men in camp at Utrecht, of whom

Napoleon's Preparations

20,000 were sent to reinforce Davout, and the garrison of Dantzig numbered over 17,000. This raised the strength of the French troops in North Germany to 130,000, who could in a short time be reinforced by over 100,000 men from the Confederation of the Rhine. By the end of 1811 Napoleon had available to deal with Russia 240,000 men, exclusive of the garrisons of Stettin and Glogau, 20,000. In December a decree was issued for 120,000 conscripts for the army and 12,000 for the fleet.

Formation of the Grand Army

The artillery parks, which had been at Augsburg and Ulm since the war with Austria in 1809, were transferred to Dantzig and the fortresses on the Oder, where there were French garrisons. Already in the spring of 1811 60,000 small arms and a considerable number of guns had been despatched to Warsaw.

The foundation of the Grand Army for the invasion of Russia was formed by Davout's corps, which was a model of organisation and administration. When Napoleon informed the Marshal that he would have to operate in a desolate country, in all probability laid waste by the enemy, and must be ready to maintain his army corps, that experienced warrior replied with an enumeration of all his preparations. His 70,000 men were provided with supplies for twenty-five days. Each company included swimmers, masons,

Davout's Corps

bakers, tailors, shoemakers, gunsmiths, in fact artificers of every description. They carried everything with them; his army was like a colony. Every want had been foreseen, and the means of supplying it prepared, even down to handmills for grinding corn.

Napoleon, finding the annual conscription insufficient to fill the ranks of his armies, took measures to collect the conscripts of previous years who had evaded service, some 60,000 in number. Movable columns were formed for this purpose and many thousands added to the army in a short time.

While negotiations with the Tzar were prolonged, the army of the Rhine was formed in rear of Davout's corps

Organisation of Armies

of observation, destined to be placed under command of Ney, recalled from Spain, and Oudinot. The Viceroy, Prince Eugene in Italy, Prince Poniatovski in the Grand Duchy of Warsaw, the King of Saxony and other princes of the Confederation of the Rhine were directed to keep their troops in readiness. Napoleon paid no less attention to the organisation of supplies, which presented great difficulties. He intended to collect in Dantzig a year's supply for 400,000 or 500,000 men.

Supplies

For this purpose General Rapp was ordered to see to the collection of wheat, and, as soon as war became inevitable, vast quantities of oats and all the hay obtainable were purchased. Dantzig,

Magdeburg and Maintz were chosen for the storage of these supplies.

Thus Napoleon succeeded in collecting vast stores of provisions and forage at a point near the prospective theatre of operations; but he had a still greater difficulty to contend with—the provision of means for the transport of these supplies with the army. There were eight **Transport** transport battalions of some 1500 biscuit waggons, drawn by four horses and requiring two drivers each, carrying three days' supplies for each battalion. Light one-horse carts, known as *chars à la comptoise*, carrying one day's supply, and bullock waggons, were obtained and organised into four battalions of one-horse carts and five battalions of ox waggons; the former were formed in Franche Compté, the latter in Lombardy, Germany and Poland. The advantage of the one-horse carts consisted in their lightness and in their requiring only one driver for several horses, which were accustomed to follow one another; while the ox waggons could move over the worst roads and the oxen required little attention and would serve for food in case of scarcity. These seventeen battalions, with 5000 or 6000 carts, were sufficient for the transport of two months' supply of food for 200,000 men. The Emperor calculated that these supplies would suffice, for the troops would subsist on the provisions collected at Dantzig and other places as far as the Niemen. Having arrived on the Niemen with 500,000 or 600,000 men, he would lead not more than 300,000 into the interior of Russia, and would then be able to feed his army, having with him forty days' supplies and utilising the resources of the country.

But 5000 or 6000 carts required 8000 or 10,000 drivers, and 18,000 or 20,000 horses and oxen; and adding to this more than 100,000 horses for the cavalry and artillery it will be understood how difficult it was to feed such a multitude of animals. Napoleon hoped to accomplish this by deferring the opening of the campaign until the appearance of grazing.

As the supply of the troops with bread instead of biscuit presents more difficulty in the grinding of the grain into flour than in the baking of bread, Napoleon directed a great part of the grain in Dantzig to be ground, while stones were obtained for the construction of ovens.

The pontoon parks were improved during the second year of preparation for war. Napoleon ordered two **Bridging Materials** parks, of 100 pontoons each, to be prepared in Dantzig. As wood for the construction of bridges could be found everywhere in the theatre of operations, while it would be much more difficult to obtain the necessary iron, cables, anchors and other materials were provided. For the carriage of all this material carts drawn by 2000 horses were provided. "With such means," wrote Napoleon, "we shall overcome all obstacles."

In the meantime the French troops of Davout, Oudinot and Ney, and the allied forces of the Confederation of the Rhine and the Grand Duchy of Warsaw were organised and supplied with everything necessary for their arduous march; and Napoleon directed Prince Eugene with the Italian army to prepare for the passage of the Alps. Counting on the friendship of Austria, he transferred to Lombardy almost all the troops remaining in Illyria and the kingdom of Naples. Three battalions were chosen from each of the best regiments, and an army of 40,000 French troops was thus formed, which, reinforced by 20,000 Italians, was detailed for the march to Russia. The remaining (4th and 5th) battalions of regiments, together with some whole regiments and Murat's Neapolitan army, were left for the defence of Italy. In addition a reserve army was formed from some Italian and Illyrian regiments, to replace the Imperial Guard and Polish troops which were to march to Russia. Among other war preparations was the organisation of 214 companies of Custom's Coastguards, which were to replace the troops guarding the coasts of France.

Preparing for an expedition to a little-known country, Napoleon made every effort to obtain all possible information about Russia, and directed the printing of a map of a hundred sheets of the western regions of Russia, with a translation of the names of places into French; this map was distributed to many of his generals. French agents in Russia, among them Prevost, Secretary of the Embassy, were directed to collect detailed statistical information regarding the Governments of Estland, Lithuania, Courland, Pskov, Vitebsk, Mohilev, Minsk, Vilna, Grodno, Bielostok, Volhynia, Kiev, Podolsk and Kherson.

His care in obtaining information about the theatre of operations is noteworthy and instructive. Thus his private secretary writes to the librarian: "I request M. Barbier to send me for his Majesty a few good books, most suitable for studying the nature of the soil of Russia, and especially of Lithuania, with respect to its marshes, rivers, forests and roads. His Majesty also desires to obtain works that treat most minutely of Charles XII.'s campaign in Poland and Russia." And again, "The Emperor requires a history of Courland, as well as all that can be obtained as to the history, geography and topography of Riga, Livonia," etc.

These measures of preparation for war, presenting us with a spectacle of the marvellous organising powers of Napoleon, are scarcely less remarkable and instructive than his strategical conceptions.

The Tzar Alexander's preparations began as soon as **Preparations of the Tzar** the designs of Napoleon became apparent, but his measures were delayed by the war with Turkey, which had been in progress several years.

These preparations included the reconnaissance of the prospective theatre of war; the strengthening of important points; the completion of the military establishment, and organisation of the reserves; the establishment of depots, magazines, hospitals and parks on a war scale. Riga, Bobruisk and Kiev were to be strengthened; Dinaburg and Sebezh, where it was intended to collect large supplies of provisions and forage, were to be fortified; fortified camps were established on the Dvina at Drissa and on the Dnieper at Kiev, and a bridge-head on the Berezina at Borisov. The greater part of these works, the fortification of Mosta on the Niemen and the construction of a *tête de pont* at Seltza on the Yasiold, for the improvement of the communications between the different parts of the army, were still in progress in the spring of 1812. But there was not time to complete all the proposed works.

During the period under review considerable additions had been made to the strength of the Russian army. Fresh units had been added to all arms, to the number of 74 battalions, 11 squadrons, 3 companies of artillery; this increase involved an augmentation of 20,000 men. The strength of the army at the beginning of 1812 amounted to 420,000 men and 1552 guns, organised as follows:—

    Infantry   . . 514 battalions
    Cavalry   . . 410 squadrons
    Artillery   . . 159 companies
    Engineers   . .   6 battalions

By June 1812 the strength was increased to 480,000 men and 1600 guns. A great part of the Russian army was scattered on the confines of the Empire when Napoleon was ready for the invasion. But the subsequent conclusion of peace with Turkey and of a treaty of alliance with Sweden, whereby considerable forces were set free to act against the invaders, must be counted among the most important of the Tzar's measures of preparation.

It will be seen that the course of the operations rendered many of the Russian magazines useless, and proved the futility of the selection of Drissa as a base for the Army of the West. Jomini tells us that there was a great divergence of opinion among the Russian generals. This, continuing throughout the campaign, led to disputes and recriminations which could not but react unfavourably on the conduct of the operations. Bagration was in **Russian Plans** favour of taking the offensive, invading the Duchy of Warsaw, and disputing the country between the Vistula and the Niemen. Barclay wished to await the enemy on the Niemen; the Prussian Staff Officer Pfuhl, who had much influence in the Russian councils, had persuaded the Tzar Alexander to construct a vast fortified camp at Drissa, on the road to St Petersburg, to which the main army was to retire and await Napoleon's decisive attack. With regard to this plan, we may quote Napoleon's dictum that "an army which remains behind its entrenchments is already beaten."

Even in those days the Press showed indiscretion in the publication of military details. Thus in the middle of June *The German Gazette* at St Petersburg published in detail the situation of all the Russian troops on the frontier from the Baltic to Slonim.

Napoleon, apparently aware of these dispositions, resolved to pass the Niemen at the salient point of Kovno, which was convenient for his project of piercing the Russian centre, and then defeat their separated forces in succession.

Napoloen's Plan

On the 9th May Napoleon left St Cloud for Dresden, where he arrived on the 16th. Here he held court such as had not been seen since the Middle Ages, attended by the kings and princes of Germany, who were made to feel his power and his superiority. A succession of splendid fêtes, concerts, and performances at the theatre, for which the élite of the actors of Paris had been brought to Dresden, formed a prelude to the great tragedy on which the curtain was about to rise. While at Dresden Napoleon heard of the Tzar's arrival at Vilna, and sent an envoy to make final overtures to Alexander. His messenger returned on the 28th May. His overtures were without result; and on the 29th May 1812 Napoleon left Dresden for the front.

Napoleon at Dresden

CHAPTER III

THE OPPOSING FORCES

The Grand Army—Character of the Army—Davout's Corps—The French Leaders—The Russian Armies—Character of the Russian Army—System of Enlistment—Martial Qualities—Russian Cavalry—Artillery—The Cossacks—Russian Officers—Staff—Administration—Russian Commanders—Position of Opposing Forces

THE army of invasion was organised as follows :—

The Grand Army — THE GRAND ARMY. THE EMPEROR NAPOLEON
Chief of the Staff—Berthier

THE GUARDS.

Old Guard	Marshal Lefebvre	10 battalions
Young Guard	Marshal Mortier	32 battalions
Legion of the Vistula		12 battalions
Cavalry	Marshal Bessières	35 squadrons
Reserve Artillery	Count Corbier	

I. CORPS.

Marshal Davout, 88 battalions, 16 squadrons

Morand	17 battalions
Friand	17 ,,
Gudin	18 ,,
Dessaix	13 ,,
Compans	23 ,,
Girardin	16 squadrons

II. CORPS.
> Marshal Oudinot, 51 battalions, 20 squadrons
>> Legrand   17 battalions
>> Verdier   15 ,,
>> Merle   19 ,,
>> Corbinot   20 squadrons

III. CORPS.
> Marshal Ney, 48 battalions, 24 squadrons
>> Ledru   17 battalions
>> Razout   17 ,,
>> Marchand   14 ,,
>> Volvart   24 squadrons

IV. CORPS.
> Prince Eugene, Viceroy of Italy, 57 battalions, 24 squadrons
>> Lechchi   5 battalions, 8 squadrons
>> Delzons   19 ,,
>> Broussier   18 ,,
>> Pino   15 ,,
>> Guion   16 squadrons

V. CORPS.
> Prince Poniatovski, 44 battalions, 20 squadrons
>> Zaionchek   16 battalions
>> Dombrovski   16 ,,
>> Kniazevich   12 ,,
>> Kaminski   20 squadrons

VI. CORPS.
> Marshal St Cyr, 28 battalions, 16 squadrons
>> Deroy   15 battalions
>> Wrede   13 ,,
>> Light Cavalry 16 squadrons

THE OPPOSING FORCES

VII. CORPS.
    Marshal Reynier, 18 battalions, 16 squadrons
        Lecoq   9 battalions
        Funck   9   ,,
        Gablentz   16 squadrons

VIII. CORPS.
    Marshal Junot, 16 battalions, 12 squadrons
        Tharreau   9 battalions
        Ochs   7   ,,
        Hamerstein 12 squadrons

IX. CORPS.
    Marshal Victor, 54 battalions, 16 squadrons
        Partouneaux 21 battalions
        Daendels   13 ,,
        Girard   20 ,,
        Fournier   16 squadrons

X. CORPS.
    Marshal Macdonald, 36 battalions, 16 squadrons
        Grandjean   16 battalions
        York   20 ,,
        Massenbach 16 squadrons

XI. (Reserve) CORPS.
    Marshal Augereau, 83 battalions, 37 squadrons

AUSTRIAN CORPS.
    Marshal Schwarzenberg, 27 battalions, 54 squadrons

CAVALRY RESERVE.
    Marshal Murat, 224 squadrons
     I. Corps Nansouty   60 squadrons
    II. Corps Montbrun   60 ,,
   III. Corps Grouchy   60 ,,
   IV. Corps Latour-Maubourg 44 ,,

Total of the Grand Army: 608,000 men and 1242 guns.

The invading army was composed of troops of various nations and unequal quality. Marbot says that "the **Character of the Army** army which crossed the Niemen amounted to 325,000 men actually present, of whom 155,000 were French." He considered that the tone of the French troops was lowered by mingling foreign regiments with them. "Thus the first corps commanded by Marshal Davout reckoned on 1st June 67,000 men, of whom 58,000 were French, the balance consisting of Germans, Spaniards and Poles. In Oudinot's corps with 34,000 French there were 1600 Portuguese, 1800 Croats and 7000 Swiss. In Ney's corps the proportion of French was even smaller, while in the fourth and sixth corps, united under Eugene Beauharnais, the French composed less than one half, the remainder being Croats, Bavarians, Spaniards, Dalmatians and Italians; and of the 44,000 cavalry under Murat 27,000 only were French . . . the foreigners all served very badly, and often paralysed the efforts of the French troops."

According to another authority twenty nations were represented in the ranks of the Grand Army. Thus out of 605 battalions of infantry, 299, comprising 224,000 men, were French, and 306 battalions, or 233,000 men, belonged to other nations. This admixture, however excellent the elements composing it may have been, did not make for efficiency in discipline or facility in command. Of the cavalry, 38,000 were French and 42,000 foreigners.

The French veteran troops had taken part in many campaigns, had attained a high state of discipline and were possessed of most warlike qualities. Their cavalry contained a great many recruits and young horses unfitted to bear the vicissitudes of a distant campaign involving many hardships.

The artillery, largely armed with 4-pounders, was inferior to that of the Russians. Many batteries were badly horsed, and in the Russian territory that was occupied scarcely any remounts were obtainable to replace the great number of animals lost from the very beginning of the campaign, involving the abandonment of guns.

The French troops, inured to war by the vicissitudes of many campaigns, well trained, well equipped, and inspired by the greatest soldier the world has ever seen, were the finest in Europe. At the same time, the superior officers were in some cases tired of war, and possibly the *moral* of the troops was not at this time quite as high as it had been, for example, during the Austerlitz Campaign.

The French were still recruited on the general system established after the Revolution; but they were far better trained, equipped and organised than when Napoleon first commanded an army in the campaign of Italy sixteen years before. The establishment of the Empire eight years previously had enhanced the power and prestige of Napoleon, whose troops were inspired by his presence.

They possessed that which is half the battle—confidence in themselves and their commanders, and in the certainty of victory. They endured fatigue and privation with remarkable constancy. They were active and enterprising, wonderful marchers, of superior intelligence, and most susceptible to appeals to their love of glory. They knew well how to adapt themselves to ground and take advantage of its natural features. The regimental officers were excellent, and constantly with their men, to whose training and well-being they devoted all their time and interest.

The cavalry consisted of heavy and light horse—cuirassiers, dragoons, hussars and mounted chasseurs. They were armed with sabre and pistol, and in some cases with carbines. Regiments were organised in four squadrons. Brigades were variable in strength. The dragoons were principally employed in reconnoitring and in outpost duties.

The artillery was generally massed, its fire being concentrated on points of attack. Co-operation between the three arms was thoroughly understood; the artillery especially had learned to give close support to the infantry. The gunners were armed with musket and bayonet. Troops were well clothed and shod, and, as will be seen, close attention was given to the commissariat, although this broke down owing to the difficulties of the campaign.

The infantry was armed with a flint gun, effective from

a hundred to two hundred yards, but ranging double that distance. In action the light troops advanced skirmishing in extended order and taking advantage of all cover; behind them followed the infantry in formed bodies in two or three lines, the attack being made generally in column. In these manœuvres, in deployments, and in skirmishing and attack in column with the bayonet, the troops had acquired great proficiency.

De Segur gives an interesting account of the interior economy of the divisions of Davout's corps, which were **Davout's Corps** a model for the rest of the army, the result being that on the march to Moscow, "they retained the fullest complement of men; their detachments, being under better discipline, brought back larger supplies, and at the same time inflicted less injury upon the inhabitants. Those who stayed with the colours lived upon the contents of their knapsacks, the clean and well-husbanded stores of which afforded relief and refreshment to the eye which was absolutely harassed by the view of the general disorder; each of these knapsacks, limited to what was strictly necessary in the articles of clothing, contained two shirts, two pairs of shoes, with nails and soles to repair them, a pair of canvas pantaloons and also of gaiters, some utensils for cleaning, a strip of linen for dressing wounds, some lint, and sixty cartridges.

"In the two sides were placed four biscuits, weighing sixteen ounces each; beneath, and at the bottom, a long and narrow canvas bag was filled with ten pounds of flour. The whole knapsack thus constituted and filled, together with the straps and oil-case covering, weighed thirty-three pounds twelve ounces.

"Each soldier carried besides, attached to a belt, a canvas bag containing two loaves weighing three pounds each. Thus with his sabre, his loaded cartridge box, three flints, turn-screw, belt and musket, he carried fifty-eight pounds' weight, and had bread for four days, biscuit for four days, flour for seven days and sixty musket-charges.

"In his rear there were carriages containing provisions for six days; but little dependence could be placed on these vehicles, which were taken up in the different places which the army came to in the state in which they were found, and would have been extremely convenient in a different country, with a smaller army and a more slow and regular system of warfare.

"When the flour-bag was empty, it was filled again with any grain that could be procured, which was ground at the first mill found on the road, or by hand-mills, which followed in the train of every regiment, or were to be met with in the villages, for these people in fact scarcely have any others. At one of these mills the labour of sixteen men was required for twelve hours to grind one day's supply of corn for a hundred and thirty men.

"In this country, every house being provided with an

oven, the army felt but little want in that respect. Bakers abounded; the regiments of the first corps comprised artisans of every description, so that victuals, clothes, everything, in short, could be prepared or mended among themselves in the course of the march. They, in fact, constituted colonies combining civilised with pastoral life. The original suggestion was the Emperor's, and Davout acted upon it. Opportunities, situations, and men had been eminently favourable to him for accomplishing the object; but the other chiefs had these elements of success less at their disposal. Besides which, their more impetuous and less methodical characters would probably have prevented their acting on the same plan with anything like the same advantage. With a genius less organising and systematic they had, therefore, greater obstacles to surmount. The Emperor had not paid sufficient attention to these distinctions, and the consequences of this neglect were highly injurious."

Most of the French generals had already borne a distinguished part in many campaigns. Jerome, the brother whom Napoleon had made King of Westphalia, was no soldier; his appointment was a mistake which had far-reaching effects, although he did not remain long with the army. Nepotism was contrary to the Emperor's practice, and prior to Austerlitz he had said: "In the army there are no princes. There are men, officers, colonels, generals, and there is a

Commander-in-Chief who must be more capable than all others and stand far above them."

Eugene de Beauharnais, Viceroy of Italy, was a brave and capable commander.

Murat, King of Naples, was a splendid leader of cavalry, possessing unsurpassed courage, activity and dash—but was no general. Ever at the head of the advanced guard, and first under fire, his appearance in front of the troops served as a signal for battle. In a green tunic heavily faced with gold and a cap with a tall red feather, surrounded by a brilliant staff including an Arab dressed as a mameluke, this fearless warrior aroused the enthusiasm of his troops and the wonder of the Cossacks, who often greeted him with cheers.

Davout was cold and methodical; although animated by the spirit of the offensive in battle, he left nothing to chance. His victory at Auerstadt, on the day of Jena, led Napoleon to refer to him in his bulletin as " of distinguished bravery, and great firmness of character, the first quality of a warrior." His services were scarcely less distinguished at Ratisbon, Eylau and Wagram. His wisdom was equally remarkable in the administration of his command and on the field of battle.

The times were favourable for, as has been truly said, only in great political cataclysms are men of character and talent likely to find a fair opportunity of rising professionally above the general dead level. Such times produced Ney, "the bravest of the brave," who had played a splendid part at Hohenlinden in 1800, and had since then been perhaps the most conspicuous figure that adorned the First Empire. He was unsurpassed as a leader of troops on the field of battle, and as a rearguard commander.

Oudinot, Victor and St Cyr were all soldiers of distinguished ability; the latter in particular possessed great intelligence and firmness of character. Napoleon considered him "the first of all of us in defensive war." He was calm amid the most exciting scenes, and had a taste for study and meditation.

Junot appeared to be suffering from the mental disease from which he perished in the succeeding year, and was no longer fit to lead troops.

Poniatovski proved himself a brave and capable leader; and there were many able soldiers among the divisional and brigade commanders.

Berthier has been characterised as a model chief-of-the-staff; but the system of Napoleon, who was in effect his own chief of the staff, had reduced Berthier to a mere automaton. He was capable of framing the orders issued by the Emperor, but not of acting on his own initiative even in minor matters.

For this Napoleon's system of centralisation was largely to blame. In the Emperor's early days, when he had smaller armies to command, and possessed unlimited energy and capacity for work, this system proved effective. But later it led to a neglect of necessary details.

The Russian Armies

The Russian forces were disposed in three armies as follows:—

FIRST WESTERN ARMY UNDER GENERAL BARCLAY DE TOLLY

1st Corps.—Lieutenant-General Count Wittgenstein: 28 battalions, 16 squadrons, 3 Cossack regiments, 9 companies artillery, 1 company pioneers, 2 pontoon companies.

2nd Corps.—Lieutenant-General Baggevoot: 24 battalions, 8 squadrons, 7 companies artillery.

3rd Corps.—Lieutenant-General Tuchkov: 24 battalions, 4 squadrons, 1 Cossack regiment, 7 companies artillery.

4th Corps.—Lieutenant-General Count Shuvalov[1]: 23 battalions, 8 squadrons, 6 companies artillery.

5th Reserve Corps.—H.I.H. the Grand Duke Constantine Pavlovich: 26 battalions, 20 squadrons, 6 companies artillery, 1 company pioneers.

6th Corps.—General Dokhturov: 24 battalions, 8 squadrons, 7 companies artillery.

1st Cavalry Corps.—Lieutenant-General Uvarov: 20 squadrons, 1 company horse artillery.

2nd Cavalry Corps.—Major-General Baron Korf: 24 squadrons, 1 company horse artillery.

3rd Cavalry Corps.—Major-General Count Palen: 24 squadrons, 1 company horse artillery.

[1] Succeeded in July by Lieutenant-General Count Osterman-Tolstoi.

Light Troops.—General Ataman Platov: 14 squadrons, 4 companies artillery.

Total: 120,000 men and 558 guns.

SECOND WESTERN ARMY UNDER GENERAL PRINCE BAGRATION

7th Corps.—Lieutenant-General Raevski: 24 battalions, 8 squadrons, 7 companies artillery.

8th Corps.—Lieutenant-General Borozdin: 22 battalions, 20 squadrons, 5 companies artillery.

4th Cavalry Corps.—Major-General Count Sivers: 24 squadrons, 1 company artillery, 1 company pioneers, 1 pontoon company.

Reserve Artillery.—4 companies.

Light Troops.—Major-General Ilovaiski: 9 Cossack regiments, 1 company artillery.

Total: 45,000 men and 216 guns.

THIRD RESERVE ARMY OF OBSERVATION GENERAL COUNT TORMASSOV

Corps.—General Count Kamenski: 18 battalions, 8 squadrons, 4 companies artillery.

Corps.—Lieutenant-General Markov: 12 battalions, 8 squadrons, 7 companies artillery.

Corps.—Lieutenant-General Baron Sacken: 12 battalions, 24 squadrons, 2 companies artillery.

Cavalry Corps.—Major-General Count Lambert: 36 squadrons.

Light Troops.—9 Cossack regiments.

Reserve Artillery.—1 artillery company, 1 pioneer company, 1 pontoon company.

Total: 46,000 men and 164 guns.

Grand total of Russian armies—211,000 men and 1038 guns. Reinforcements joined later, including the army of Moldavia under Admiral Chichagov, set free by the treaty with Turkey, and the army of Finland under General Steinheil.

Of the character of the Russian army, Sir Robert Wilson, who knew it well at this period, wrote: "The **Character of the Russian Army** infantry is generally composed of athletic men between the ages of eighteen and forty, endowed with great bodily strength, but generally of short stature, with martial countenance and complexion; inured to the extremes of weather and hardships; to the worst and scantiest food; to marches for days and nights, of four hours' repose and six hours' progress; accustomed to laborious toils and the carriage of heavy burthens; ferocious, but disciplined; obstinately brave, and susceptible of enthusiastic excitements; devoted to their sovereign, their chief, and their country. Religious without being weakened by superstition; patient, docile, and obedient; possessing all the energetic characteristics of a barbarian people, with the advantages grafted by civilisation."

A system of compulsory service ensured the enlistment of the best men. The magistrates selected the most **System of Enlistment** efficient young men according to the required number. The Russian soldier was thus selected from a numerous population, with the greatest attention to his physical powers; no man even with bad teeth was enlisted.

In accordance with the traditions of Suvarov, the bayonet was the principal weapon of the Russian infantry.

Martial Qualities The French had already experienced their fighting powers in the campaign of Austerlitz, and at Friedland and Eylau in 1807. The regiments of light infantry, and especially the chasseurs of the Guard, composed largely of men from Siberia, were hardy, excellently trained, and good marksmen. The footguards, numbering some 7000 men, were the élite of the army, of whom Sir R. Wilson wrote—"there cannot be a nobler corps, or one of more warlike description."

The Russian cavalry was said by the same authority to be the best mounted on the Continent, "and as **Russian Cavalry** English horses can never serve abroad in English condition,[1] it is the best mounted in Europe." After the battle of Eylau, when the Imperial cavalry of the guards were ordered from St Petersburg to join the army in Poland, the men were sent in waggons as far as Riga, and the horses accompanied at the rate of fifty miles each day. From thence they were ridden thirty-five miles a day for 700 miles, and arrived in good condition.

The cavalry soldiers were brave and intelligent, and

[1] "At least as long as the English cavalry are nurtured to require warm stables, luxuriant beds, etc.—so long as efficiency abroad is sacrificed to appearance at home."—Sir R. WILSON.

had especially distinguished themselves at the battles of Eylau and Friedland, where they covered the retreat of the infantry.

The Russians were strong in artillery, and their guns were well equipped and well served. Four horses drew the light field-pieces and eight and twelve pounders. The drivers were of high quality, and the artillery was remarkably mobile, and, although they did not attach too much reputation or disgrace to the possession or loss of a gun, few guns were lost in the campaign in Poland.

Artillery

The Cossacks, natives of the Don and Volga, merit some notice in an account of a campaign in which they bore a conspicuous part. Living in semi-independence, under their own laws, and exempt from taxes, the Cossacks were under an obligation to serve for five years with the Russian army. They were born soldiers who with their first accents learn to lisp of war. From eight years of age the boys rode fearlessly over the steppe on half-wild, bare-backed horses. On holidays they fired at marks, cut posts, and indulged in various warlike games, while the long evenings were passed in listening to tales of raids and adventures with which the veterans fired the spirits of their sons. Armed with long lances, guns, sabres and pistols, they rode small but hardy horses; lightly equipped, a snaffle, halter, the tree of a saddle, on which was bound a cushion

The Cossacks

stuffed with the Cossack's property, on which he rode, formed the whole of his baggage.

Count Benkendorf, who was employed with Cossacks, wrote in 1816: "The Cossack is born with that degree of activity, intelligence, and enterprise that up to the rank of non-commissioned officer he is unrivalled; but he degenerates immediately when he is pushed beyond his place into a higher grade. The non-commissioned officers are the soul of a regiment of the Don, because they almost always obtain that advancement owing to their own merit." No troops were better adapted for night marches than the Cossacks. Their sabres were firmly fixed in their girdles; they had no spurs; and no metal to clash against their arms. The stars served them as guides; and they would get supplies and forage for their horses where other troops would starve. Cossack movements were very simple, and they had their own peculiar tactics. They generally marched in sections of threes. The squadron (*sotnia*) standards were united at the head of the column; the squadron leaders in front and the other officers on the flank. In deploying they formed up in single rank. A close column was rapidly reformed on the centre. Their principal tactical manœuvre was the celebrated *lava*, learnt from the Tartar hordes of Ghengiz Khan and Taimur, and from the bitter experience of many a bloody fight. This consisted in fighting in a loose formation, tiring out their foes, and drawing them into ambuscades. Writing in this year of 1812, the French Marshal Morand said : " We (the French cavalry) deploy, and boldly advance to the attack, and already reach their line ; but they disappear like a dream and we see only the bare pines and birch trees. An hour later, when we have begun to feed our horses, the dark line of Cossacks again appears on the horizon, and we are again threatened with an onslaught. We repeat the same manœuvre, and, as before, our operations are not attended with success. Thus one of the best and bravest cavalry forces the world has ever seen was tired out and disorganised by those whom it considered unworthy foes, but who were the real saviours of their country." Again, Bronzevski wrote : " In the day of trial the Don Cossacks stood in the first rank of the defenders of their country. The great deeds performed by them in the war of the fatherland form the golden epoch of their history, and surpass all the glory and renown won by them in former campaigns."

They do not appear, however, to have been much more than efficient skirmishers, and in the attack they displayed little enterprise and no high order of courage. But their elusive tactics wore out their opponents.

With the exception of those of the Guards and cavalry, the officers of the Russian army had generally little education, a circumstance which reacted especially on the efficiency of the infantry of the line. But their courage was unimpeachable, and

Russian Officers

they were ready to undergo any hardship in the service of their country. The superior officers, drawn generally from the Guards, were highly educated and usually acquainted with several languages. In 1807 Sir R. Wilson wrote: "Amongst the present Russian officers there is no deficiency of talent; there are indeed many excellent generals of brigade and division, but an uninterrupted succession of Suvarovs cannot be expected."

The staff was generally untrained and inefficient, although the officers of the Quartermaster-General's Department could draw well, rapidly, and accurately, and take up ground quickly and judiciously. But their duties were too complicated and there was a lack of proper chiefs. Great attention was paid to departmental minutiæ, and "the lowest Cossack officer from his saddle on the snow was obliged to send his information with such care about the paper, wording, folding and address, as if the report was destined to be preserved in the archives of St Petersburg."

Staff

The administrative departments generally were greatly neglected in the Russian army, especially those of commisariat and transport, although no soldier in Europe was satisfied more easily than the Russian, while excellent transport was obtainable in the two-horse Russian *Kibitka*. During the campaign in Poland in 1807 the Russian army was reduced to the verge of starvation. The medical department was no

Administration

better, for want of an efficient staff. The wounded were for the first time dressed on the field of battle at Friedland.

In every respect the Russians had gained valuable experience in the wars with Napoleon, and the army was now the most formidable with which the great conqueror had had to contend.

The Russians had experienced and capable generals, many of whom had previously met the French at Austerlitz and in Poland. Barclay de Tolly, Minister of War, who commanded the First Western Army, was cool, straightforward and steadfast. He had exerted himself in army reform, and made enemies in the process. His want of confidence in others led him to the performance of many duties which might have been carried out by subordinates. Like so many distinguished Russians, he was of foreign extraction; he was regarded with some distrust as a foreigner, and had not sufficient command of the language to converse with the Russian soldiers.

Russian Commanders

Prince Bagration, Commander of the Second Army, was a born warrior who had served under Suvarov, and fought in the Caucasus, in Turkey, Poland, Italy, Austria and Finland, where he had distinguished himself in every action. Always with the advanced guard or the rearguard, Bagration was tireless in war. Considerate to others, strict towards himself, he knew, like Suvarov, the value of those under his command. All who surrounded him were devoted in his service. He was not as well educated as Barclay in theory and in administration, but he was more able to inspire his troops.

Tormassov, before his appointment to the command of the Third Army, was known as a skilful military administrator, with a gift for diplomacy, exhibited a short time before in war with the Turks, and Persians, when he was Commander-in-Chief of the troops in Gruzia and on the line of the Caucasus. Unable to beat his enemy in the field, he had cunningly kept the Turks and Persians apart. He was strict in his relations with his subordinates, regarding zealous service as a duty, and not as entailing a right to distinction or reward.

Count Lambert, who throughout the war generally commanded the advanced guard, first with Tormassov and afterwards with Chichagov, was a Frenchman who had left his native country in his youth and entered the Russian service. He had distinguished himself and was severely wounded in the war of 1799, and in the campaign of 1807 he had gained renown as a cavalry general and advanced guard commander.

Count Wittgenstein, then forty-four years old, was a bold and active warrior, not highly educated, but with capacity for command and ability to inspire his troops by his example, while the devotion of his staff helped to render him a formidable opponent.

Kutuzov, who was on the 20th August 1812 appointed

to the command of all the Russian armies, was sixty-seven years of age, and had scarcely the energy of body and mind requisite for the task before him. The Napoleonic wars had already shown the value of youth in the commanders of armies; the failure of Napoleon's adversaries, and the signs of decline in himself, point to the essential truth of his own dictum that " no general has any enterprise after his forty-fifth year."

Kutuzov was inferior to Barclay de Tolly in administrative ability, and to Bagration in activity. He was experienced and cunning but somewhat dilatory and unenterprising. He had, however, the confidence of the whole army and nation, which was lost by Barclay owing to his prolonged retreat, and was thus an asset of value.

Miloradovich, possessing many of the qualities of a fine advanced guard commander, tireless, cool and cheerful in the midst of danger, was, however, neglectful of the proper disposition of his troops, and some of his orders were scarcely intelligible. But he was always to be found at the post of danger.

There were many other good commanders among the Russians—Osterman, Prince Eugene of Wurtemburg, Konovnitzin, Baggevoot, Platov, Ataman of Cossacks, and the brothers Tuchkov.

Positions of Opposing Armies When the campaign opened on the 23rd June 1812 the opposing armies were posted as follows:—

RUSSIANS

FIRST ARMY.—Barclay de Tolly, 120,000 men and 558 guns. Headquarters at Vilna

1st Corps.—Wittgenstein, at Kedani; detachment at Rossiana; advanced guard at Yurbourg.

2nd Corps.—Baggevoot, at Orzhishki; advanced guard at Yanovo.

3rd Corps.—Tuchkov, at Novia Troki; advanced guard at Visoki Dvor.

4th Corps.—Shuvalov, at Olkeniki; advanced guard at Orani.

5th Corps.—Grand Duke Constantine Pavlovich, at Sventziani.

6th Corps.—Dokhturov, at Lida; advanced guard formed by the 3rd Cavalry Reserve Corps under Palen at Lebiuda.

1st Reserve Cavalry Corps.—Uvarov, at Vilkomir.
2nd Reserve Cavalry Corps.—Baron Korf, at Smorgoni.

The last two cavalry corps formed the second line of the First Army. Platov's flying detachment was at Grodno.

SECOND ARMY.—Bagration, 45,000 men and 216 guns, between the Niemen and the Bug, with headquarters at Volkovisk.

7th Corps.—Raevski, at Novi Dvor.
8th Corps.—Borozdin, at Volkovisk.
4th Cavalry Reserve Corps.—Sievers, at Zelva.
Flying Detachment.—Ilovaiski, at Bielostok.

THIRD ARMY.—Tormassov, in Volhynia. Headquarters at Lutzk

FRENCH

NAPOLEON.—Headquarters at Vilkovishki

Guard.—At Vilkovishki.
1st Corps.—Davout, forest of Pilviski.
2nd Corps.—Oudinot, in rear.
3rd Corps.—Ney, in advance at Marienpol.
4th Corps.—Eugene, at Oletzko.
6th Corps.—Gouvion St Cyr, at Tzimochen.
1st Cavalry Reserve Corps.—Nansouty ⎫
2nd ,, ,, ,, Montbrun ⎬ Between Kovno and Preni.
3rd ,, ,, ,, Grouchy ⎭

RIGHT WING.—King Jerome. Headquarters at Augustovo

5th Corps.—Poniatovski, at Augustovo.
7th Corps.—Reynier, at Ostrolenko.
8th Corps.—Vandamme, at Augustovo.

These corps arrived at their destination on the 25th June.

4th Cavalry Corps.—Latour Manbourg, at Augustovo.
LEFT WING.—Macdonald, Tilsit.

CHAPTER IV

THE THEATRE OF WAR

THE western regions of Russia and the strip of country from the Upper Dnieper to Moscow formed the theatre of the war of 1812. Generally the whole western portion of the Russian empire, bounded on the north by the Baltic Sea, on the west by the Niemen and Bug, on the south by the Dniester and on the east by the Dnieper and Dwina may be divided into three parts : 1. The *Northern*, from the Baltic to the forest region.[1] 2. The *Central*, including the forest region, together with the marshes of the Berezina and the Bielovezh plain. 3. The *Southern*, from the forest region to the Dniester and the Austrian frontier.

The northern portion is undulating, intersected by rivers which do not present formidable obstacles to the passage of troops, in parts covered with forests, lakes and inextensive marshes; the borderland of the Baltic Sea has a surface soil of clay, sand and black earth, and is fairly productive; the part nearest the forest region is for the greater part sandy. The region on the right bank

[1] In Russian *polyesiyé*—forest region.

of the Lower Dwina is covered by innumerable lakes, marshes, forests, small hills and streams, which fall into the Dwina; of these streams the most important is the Drissa, which by its direction, parallel to the course of the Dwina, and owing to the left bank commanding the right, presents an advantageous defensive line against an enemy crossing the Dwina between the town of Drissa and the mouth of the River Ula. The region from Smolensk to Moscow, forming the theatre of operations of Napoleon's Grand Army, as it approaches the ancient capital, becomes more and more open; the country is fertile and well cultivated, and abounds in wheat and other supplies necessary for an army.

The forest region, the country lying in the form of a triangle between Brest-Litovsk, Rogachev and the mouth of the Pripet, presents a strip of low-lying, marshy ground covered with dense forests, in the midst of which small open spaces are met with, characterised by sandy hills, and valleys suited for cultivation, in which are a few villages. All the rivers of this region flow between low, marshy banks, and in spring and autumn overflow for a considerable distance, when they become impassable, or can be crossed only slowly by means of flat-bottomed boats and rafts. It will be understood then that, in the first place, the forest region divides the northern and southern parts of the western borderland of the Empire; and in the second place, that that country is specially suitable for the operations of partisan detachments, all the more because the sparse population and absence of supplies does not admit of the employment of considerable forces.

Finally the southern portion of the western borderland of Russia presents a low terrain, partly marshy, or undulating and covered with forest; the rivers flowing into the Pripet, of which the principal are the Styr and Gorin, have for the most part low banks, but constitute sufficiently advantageous defensive lines, which in 1812 were secured on the left flank by the neutrality of Galicia, for although the Austrian Government supplied Napoleon with an army corps, they did not declare war on Russia. The country south of the forest region includes Volhynia and Podolia, which belong to the most fertile part of the Empire.

The River Niemen formed the first obstacle to Napoleon's advance across the northern part of Western Russia, which comprised the chief theatre of operations; but that defensive line was unfavourable for the Russians, as the left bank is commanded by the right for almost the whole course of the river below Grodno. The width of the Niemen above Kovno is from 250 to 300 paces, and below Kovno from 350 to 400 paces. There were bridges across the river at Novo-Sverzhen, Bielitza, Mosti, Grodno and Tilsit; ferries at Kovno, Yurburg and other places. The second considerable obstacle in the direction of St Petersburg was the Western Dwina, and towards Moscow—the Berezina and the Upper Dnieper. The Western Dwina presents a highly advantageous defensive line, strengthened at its lower end by the fortress of Riga (the fortifications of Dinaburg had scarcely been begun). Moreover, a hundred versts above Dinaburg, on the left bank of the Dwina, a fortified camp was established at Drissa, in which it was proposed to concentrate the main strength of the Russian army. Above Dinaburg the Dwina does not present any considerable obstacle, for the banks are low and the depth is not great, and during a dry summer fords appear. From Vitebsk to Drissa, and for some distance below the latter point, the left bank commands the right; farther on, to Riga itself, the right bank is higher than the left. The width of the river between Vitebsk and Dinaburg in from 180 to 230 paces, and at Riga, 800 paces. There were bridges at Velizh, Surazh, Vitebsk, Dinaburg and Riga; and ferries at Budilova, Bieshenkovichy, Ula, Polotzk, Disna, Drissa, Leonpol, Druya, Jacobstadt and Friedrichstadt.

The River Berezina might serve as a defensive line to cover the front between the Dwina and the Dnieper. That region extends from Vitebsk to Orsha, 60 versts; and in width presents a marshy and wooded strip, extending on one side to Syenno, and on the other to Poryechiye and Smolensk. The region between the Berezina and the Dnieper is still more enclosed and resembles the forest region. The supporting points of the defensive line on the Berezina in 1812 were furnished by the fortresses of Bobruisk and Borisov, but the first of these lay to one side of the main roads to the interior, and could therefore not exercise a decisive influence on the operations; the stronghold of Borisov, for want of time, could not be brought into use, for the engineering works were confined to the arming of the bridge-head. The width of the Berezina from the canal to its junction with the Dnieper varied from 60 to 120 paces. The right bank commands the left, except at Veselovo, Studianka, Borisov and Nijni-Berezina, where the left bank is higher than the right. Fords are to be found in summer and sometimes in autumn, but generally the passage is rendered difficult by marshes extending on both banks of the river. There were bridges at Borisov and Bobruisk; ferries at Veselovo, Nijni-Berezina, and other places.

The River Dnieper, flowing from Dorogobuzh to Orsha, almost parallel with the Western Dwina, and beyond Orsha sharply turning to the south, although navigable throughout its whole course from Dorogobuzh to its mouth, cannot be said to furnish a favourable defensive line against an enemy advancing on Moscow, not only because at many points the right bank commands the left, but because during summer fords are to be found above Smolensk, at Lyada, Khomino, Mohilev, Vorkolabov, Novi-Bikhov, and other places. The width of the river at Dorogobuzh is 90 paces, from Smolensk to Stari-Bikhov 100 to 150 paces, and below Bikhov to its junction with the Pripet gradually increases to 500 paces. There were bridges at Smolensk, Mohilev and Kiev; ferries at many points. The fortified town of Smolensk, lying at the junction of the roads from Poryechiye, Vitebsk, Orsha, Mstislavl, Roslavl, Dorogobuzh and Dukhovshchina, affords means for a stubborn defence.

The first line of defence against the irruption of an enemy into the southern region is formed by the Western Bug. The width of this river at Ustilug is about 40 paces, and at Drogichin, 120 paces. In summer many fords are to be found between Vlodava and Brest. Generally, the left bank commands the right, except at points at Ustilug, Opalin, Brest, Nemirov and Drogichin, where the right bank is the higher. Much better lines of defence are furnished by the Rivers Styr and Gorin.

Generally in the districts to the north and south of the forest region there were a great many roads, mutually intersecting one another in every direction; but their condition varied with the weather and the time of year. On these roads it was impossible to employ, with constant success, the transport used in the Napoleonic armies in Germany and Italy; and light transport required a multitude of horses to carry supplies for the troops, which in their turn were with difficulty supplied with forage, of which there was not always sufficient even for the troop-horses of the immense army of invasion.

In the forest region the number of roads was strictly limited, and generally communications were difficult, especially in spring and autumn.

The climate of Russia is characterised by extreme cold in winter, which comes on very rapidly, and considerable heat in summer. During the first part of the campaign the invading armies suffered much from sultry weather as well as from heavy rain; while during the retreat they were destroyed by the cold. The effect of climate is thus expressed by Napier, who wrote: "What vast preparations, what astonishing combinations were involved in the plan, what vigour and ability displayed in the execution of Napoleon's march to Moscow! Yet when winter came, only four days sooner than he expected, the giant's scheme became a theme for children's laughter!" In fact, the forces of Nature with which the invaders had to contend were more terrible and imposing than the hostility of man.

CHAPTER V

THE INVASION OF LITHUANIA

General Distribution—Russians—French—Napoleon on the Niemen—Forward Movement—Passage of the River—Napoleon's Plan—Further Advance—The Russians surprised—General Russian Retreat—French Advance—Napoleon's Dispositions—Movements of the King of Westphalia—Bagration's Retreat—Pursuit of Bagration—Weather Conditions—Difficulties of Supply and Transport—Comments

WHEN the French Emperor left Dresden on the 28th May the Russian armies were distributed on a wide front, with a view to meeting the enemy wherever his attack developed.

General Distribution

The First Army—Barclay de Tolly—120,000 men and 558 guns, with headquarters at Vilna, and flanks at Rossiana and Lida.

Russians

Second Army—Bagration—45,000 men and 216 guns, with headquarters at Volkovisk, lay between that place and Bielostok near the Bug.

Third Army—Tormassov—46,000 men and 164 guns, was in Volhynia, with headquarters at Lutzk.

On that date Napoleon's army was standing on the Vistula, so disposed that an advance could be made from either wing with equal facility.

French

Napoleon's plan was to pierce the too extended Russian line by a movement on Vilna, and then defeat the enemy in detail. It was in accord with the principle he had carried out with success in Italy and in Spain, and was yet to adopt in the Waterloo campaign. He would "concentrate 400,000 men on one point."

On the morning of the 23rd June 1812 a travelling carriage, drawn by six horses and accompanied by an **Napoleon on the Niemen** escort of mounted chasseurs of the Guard, drew up near a regiment of Polish Lancers on the outposts near the bank of the Niemen opposite Kovno. Napoleon alighted from the carriage, and questioned the officers who approached as to the routes to the Niemen. He expressed a desire to put on a Polish uniform, and donned Colonel Pogovski's cloak and forage cap. Accompanied by Berthier and one of the Polish officers he rode to the advanced posts, to the village of Alexoten, opposite Kovno; afterwards, with General Haxo, his Engineer Commander, having carefully observed the locality, he rode higher up the Niemen to the village of Ponyemun, where Haxo found a very convenient point of passage, where a bend in the river would facilitate the concentration of the fire of batteries posted on the left bank. Napoleon reconnoitred the place, without being observed; some Cossack patrols were the only troops visible on the farther bank of the Niemen. At one point his horse stumbled and threw him on the sand, as he or one of his suite remarked : " A bad omen ! A Roman would have turned back." Returning from this reconnaissance, the Emperor was very gay, and during the day frequently hummed the old air : " Marlbrouk s'en va-t-en guerre."

Afterwards, having discarded the Polish garments, he proceeded to Nogarishki, a village lying six versts from Kovno, somewhat to the right of the road from Vilkovishki to that place.

On this day Napoleon's main army, consisting of the corps of Davout, Oudinot, Ney, Nansouty, Montbrun and the Guard, to the number of 220,000 men, approached the Niemen in the neighbourhood of Kovno ; and Macdonald reached Tilsit with 32,500.

Forward Movement

At the same time the Viceroy Eugene, St Cyr, and Grouchy moved on Kalvaria and Preni ; King Jerome, with the corps of Poniatovski, Reynier, Vandamme and Latour-Maubourg, also numbering some 80,000, marched on Bielostok and Grodno ; while Schwarzenberg marched towards Drogichin on the Bug with 34,000 men.

Napoleon's headquarters were established at Nogarishki. Arrived there, he issued orders for the passage of the Niemen, for which three pontoon bridges of 75 pontoons each were to be constructed at Ponyemun, at intervals of not less than 150 paces. In addition a fourth bridge was to be thrown across at Alexoten, where the pontoons were to remain until the French troops had occupied

Kovno, and afterwards serve for the crossing of the main road between that town and Alexoten. The orders showed in detail the disposition of the troops up to and for the passage, the situation of the batteries, and the order of march of the columns on the farther bank of the river.

At nine o'clock in the evening Napoleon again went to Ponyemun, where the work was begun in his presence. Some boats found on the left bank of the river served for the passage of three companies of the 13th Light Infantry, **Passage of the River** which at once occupied an adjacent village; a Cossack patrol retired after exchanging a few shots. By midnight the French army was already moving across the bridges, and as they reached the farther bank they formed up in deep columns. Davout's corps marched on by the road leading through Zhizhmori to Vilna, and Murat's cavalry followed.

Napoleon's plan was to pierce the Russian centre with the Guards, the corps of Davout, Oudinot, Ney and **Napoleon's Plan** Murat with Nansouty and Montbrun's cavalry, moving from Kovno on Vilna, the first objective of the campaign. This movement would be supported on the right rear by Eugene with the 4th Corps together with St Cyr's corps and Grouchy's cavalry; while, farther back again on the right rear, the Emperor's brother, Jerome, King of Westphalia, would advance with the right wing, and distract the attention of the Russians from the main line of advance. Should the enemy assume the offensive in the direction of Warsaw, Jerome would stand on the defensive, while Eugene attacked them in flank, and the Emperor, descending from Vilna, would sever them from their base. The main attacking army thus advanced across the Niemen between Grodno and Kovno. The two extreme flanks of this great army of invasion were covered—the left by Macdonald, who would advance from Tilsit on Rossiana, the right by Schwarzenberg, towards Lublin.

Napoleon established his headquarters at Kovno on the 24th June. Learning that Prince Eugene would not **Further** arrive at Kalvaria until the 26th, and dreading **Advance** to expose Ney alone to the attacks of the Russian forces which he supposed to be at Troki, the Emperor decided to bring Ney's corps to Kovno. At the same time, in order to secure both banks of the Vilia, he directed Oudinot to throw a bridge across that river, and send over a division and some cavalry; and Macdonald was ordered to enter into communication with Oudinot, which was established by Grandjean's division at Georgenburg.

These dispositions were made in case of a Russian offensive movement against the left flank of the army, the corps of Ney and Oudinot being disposed to ward off this danger. The right wing under King Jerome was directed on Grodno, where it would pass the Niemen on

THE INVASION OF LITHUANIA   53

the 29th June. Schwarzenberg was to unite with Reynier towards Slonim.

The news that the French army had crossed the Niemen reached Vilna on the night of the 24th June. The celerity of the movement in passing 200,000 men across the river in the course of a few hours was a surprise to the Russians, although they had already taken the precaution to move their archives and treasure. The Emperor Alexander left Vilna on the morning of the 26th, when Barclay de Tolly concentrated the 3rd and 4th Corps at that place. But as the enemy advanced, and came in contact with his advanced troops, Barclay was obliged to retire and withdrew to Sventziani on the 28th, directing Baggevoot to delay the enemy at Shirvinti. He had already sent directions to General Dorokhov, who was at Orani, to retire on Mikhalishki; and Platov was ordered to retreat from Grodno through Lida and Smorgoni towards Sventziani, opposing the enemy wherever possible and laying waste the country on his route. At the same time, informing Bagration of his retreat with the 3rd and 4th Corps on Sventziani, he instructed him "to conform to this movement, taking care that the enemy did not cut his communications via Minsk with Borisov and to guard his right flank," and keep up communication with Platov and Tormassov. All stores that could not be carried away from Vilna

The Russians surprised

General Russian Retreat

were burnt, and the bridges over the Vilia were destroyed. Simultaneously Wittgenstein retired with the 1st Corps on Vilkomir; Korf's cavalry retreated from Smorgoni on Mikhalishki; and Dokhturov with the 6th Corps on Smorgoni. The whole of the First Russian Army was thus in full retreat; but Bagration was still at Volkovisk.

Napoleon reached Vilna on the 28th June, making a state entry, when he was received with acclamation by the Polish populace.

Oudinot reached Vilkomir the same day, driving out Wittgenstein's rearguard; Ney was advancing along the right bank of the Vilia, and Macdonald advanced through Rossiana. Eugene was at Preni, on the left bank of the Niemen, and received orders to advance on Vilna; and Jerome, who was at Augustovo, was directed to move at once on Grodno, where Latour-Maubourg had already arrived with his cavalry. Schwarzenberg was at Siedlitz.

French Advance

The movement on Vilna had thus pierced the Russian centre, and separated their First and Second Armies. Reviewing the situation at Vilna, Napoleon, though not clear as to Bagration's position, now perceived the opportunity of cutting off and destroying that general's army. He despatched Murat in pursuit of the main body of Barclay de Tolly, toward Sventziani, with the cavalry and two of Davout's divisions. Nansouty, with his cavalry and one of

Napoleon's Dispositions

Davout's divisions, was sent towards Mikhalishki to deal with Dokhturov; and Davout, with his two remaining divisions, Grouchy's cavalry, and a Polish division, moved on Volozhin to cut in on the line of retreat of the Second Russian Army. King Jerome, with the right wing of the army, was supposed to be following up Bagration, in order that, in conjunction with Davout, he might destroy his army.

Movements of the King of Westphalia

But Jerome was dilatory in his movements. His cavalry patrols had been before Grodno since the 23rd June, but he himself did not enter that place until the 30th, when he arrived with a division of the 5th Corps. He spent some days in concentrating and in attending to his commissariat. Instead of making every effort to gain contact with Bagration, he remained inactive, apparently awaiting orders from Vilna, and sending no information to the Emperor's headquarters. He allowed Bagration to retreat unmolested, and as Napoleon wrote to him on the 4th July, "compromised all the success of the campaign on the right. It is impossible to wage war thus."

Meanwhile Bagration left Volkovisk on the 28th June, collected his corps at Zelva by the 30th, and next day continued his march to Slonim. Continuing his retreat in accordance with Barclay's instructions, Bagration reached Novogrudok on the 3rd July, and passed the Niemen at Nikolaev on the 4th

Bagration's Retreat

and 5th, with the intention of marching on Vileika. But hearing from Platov that Davout was at Vishnev with an army said to be 60,000 strong, and having information of the enemy's appearance at Zelva in his rear and in the direction of Grodno on his flank, he recrossed the river, intending to march by Novi-Sverzhen on Minsk, and assembled his forces at Karlichi. Hearing from Platov that he had communication with Dorokhov, who had reached Kamen, he directed him and that general to occupy Volozhin and effect a junction with him (Bagration) at Minsk. But on arriving next day at Mir, Bagration heard from Dorokhov that the French were in great force at Minsk, and, wishing to avoid a general action, according to his instructions, he again changed his route, taking the road by Nyesvizh and Slutzk to Bobruisk. On the 8th July the whole of his army was concentrated at Nyesvizh. Platov with his Cossack flying column reached Mir on the 9th, and there made a stand against the enemy's advanced cavalry, afterwards continuing to cover the retreat of Bagration's army through Slutzk on 13th, and Bobruisk.

King Jerome had not sent his cavalry on under Latour-Maubourg from Grodno until 4th July, and this was at **Pursuit of Bagration** Novogrudok on the 8th, the same day that Davout reached Minsk, for the enemy whom Bagration had heard of at that place were only advanced troops.

Jerome reached Novogrudok with two corps on the 11th, and Nyesvizh on the 14th, his other two corps following and watching their right flank, exposed to Tormassov in Volhynia. But Bagration, although he had not yet effected a junction with the First Army, had escaped the danger of being surrounded by Davout and Jerome. Schwarzenberg was now at Prushani and Reynier approaching Slonim. Eugene, nearing Smorgoni, was in a position to join either Jerome or Davout.

During this period the troops had suffered much from the extraordinary heat which set in in the early days of July; many officers and men succumbed, while the Emperor himself was prostrated. This weather, and the heavy rain that preceded it, was among the causes of the slowness of Jerome's movements, while at every point difficulties of supply and transport were met with. Owing to the state of the roads from rain towards the end of June the baggage could not keep up with the troops, and not only supplies, but transport to enable them to follow the army, had to be provided at Grodno. The troops had to subsist mainly on meat alone. It was not until the 10th July that Jerome was able to assemble his main army, reduced to a strength of 45,000 men, at Nyesvizh, distant 200 versts from Grodno, and he considered it necessary to keep his troops concentrated, as Bagration was falsely reported to be have 100,000 men.

Weather Conditions

Want of provisions and forage was experienced immediately after the crossing of the Niemen. Thousands of horses died from being fed on green corn. The army, ill supplied with provisions, lived on the scanty resources of the country, and the men took to plunder and insubordination, which undermined discipline and resulted in large numbers of stragglers. Immense convoys of bullocks had followed the army, the greater number in droves, others harnessed to the provision waggons; but while many reached Vilna and Minsk, few got so far as Smolensk; they could not keep up with the armies. While Dantzig contained enough grain to supply the army, the rivers had been depended upon for transporting it. But the Vilna was so dried up as to be unnavigable for the lighters. An attempt was made to organise a transport corps of Lithuanian carriages at Vilna, where 500 were collected, but they proved useless. By the time the provisions which had been stopped at Kovno reached Vilna, the army had left that place.

Difficulties of Supply and Transport

Napoleon's first great manœuvre—the piercing of the Russian line and the consequent separation of their forces—was successfully completed when his centre crossed the Niemen and advanced to Vilna. But with Bagration's escape from a combined attack by the armies of Davout and Jerome, which must have crushed him out of existence, the second part of the

Comments

CHAPTER VI

THE ADVANCE TO THE DWINA

Napoleon's Plan—The Russians at Drissa—Oudinot's Advance—Macdonald's Movements—Napoleon leaves Vilna—The Movement towards Vitebsk—Action at Ostrovno—Napoleon at Ostrovno—Operations at Vitebsk—Forward Movement—Operations against Bagration—Oudinot and Wittgenstein—Movements of Schwarzenberg—Comments

Napoleon's Plan

WHEN he realised that Bagration had escaped, Napoleon planned to follow Barclay de Tolly with the corps of Murat, Ney and Oudinot, whilst Eugene and Davout, the latter now in command of Jerome's army, advanced on Polotzk and Vitebsk, to threaten the Russian line of communications with St Petersburg and Moscow.

The Russians at Drissa

The First Russian Army had retreated to the Dwina and occupied the fortified camp of Drissa between the 9th and 11th July. But that camp was untenable. Its strategical situation, to one side of all the main roads leading into the interior, rendered it useless, while it was faulty also from a tactical point of view, being situated in a bend on the west side of the River Dwina, and in close proximity to an extensive forest, under cover of which an enemy could mass his forces.

The Tzar had been with Barclay at Polotzk, where he left the army in order to go to St Petersburg and Moscow, to excite the nation to a general armament and resistance, and to organise a militia.

Considering the Drissa camp untenable, Barclay de Tolly evacuated it, crossed the Dwina on the 14th July, and took up a position on the right bank of the river, while his cavalry later engaged that of the advancing French.

This day Napoleon was still at Vilna. Murat, with the head of the Centre Army, had advanced by Vidzy to Zamosha, his cavalry being pushed forward towards Drissa and Druya. Ney, following in support, reached Drisviati. Oudinot reconnoitred Dinaburg, decided **Oudinot's Advance** that the loss that would be entailed in attacking it would be too great, and turned up the left bank of the Dwina in the direction of Druya. His advance on Dinaburg elicited a reproof from Napoleon: "The Emperor has viewed with astonishment and regret your movement on Dinaburg without orders. If you supposed the Russian army to be there, you exposed your corps without reason. If you knew the Russian army was not there, your march is still more blameable; you exposed your right to attack from Drissa. The Emperor ordered you to go to Solok."

Macdonald, in accordance with instructions issued on the 9th July, was to march on Jacobstadt and Friedrichstadt, and threaten to pass the Dwina there. He had reached Ponyeviezh. He was told that the first object of his corps was to protect the navigation of the Niemen; his second—to contain the garrison of Riga "consisting of thirty battalions of this year's recruits and unworthy of consideration"; his third—to pass the Drissa between Riga and Dinaburg, to disturb the enemy; his fourth—to occupy Courland, and preserve that province intact since it held so many supplies for the army; finally, as soon as the right moment arrived, to pass the Dwina, blockade Riga, to call up the siege train and begin the siege of that place, which was important to secure winter quarters and to give a point of support on this great river. These were "not positive orders but only general instructions, because the distance is very great and will become greater."

Macdonald's Movements

Jerome was this day, 14th July, at Nyesvizh; he received orders placing him under Davout, and he resigned his command. The cavalry of Latour-Maubourg was in advance. Schwarzenburg was at Ruzhani. Bagration, retreating before this advance, had left Slutzk for Bobruisk; Davout was approaching Mohilev. Tormassov was at Lutzk, and Reynier was ordered back from Nyesvizh to cover Poland.

The general effect of all these movements will be

E

observed to be—a concentration of the Russian armies towards Vitebsk and Smolensk, to cover Moscow; and a general advance of the French in pursuit, clearing the country as they proceeded, and providing for the protection of flanks and rear.

Napoleon's plan was to operate with his right, avoiding any attack on Dinaburg and Drissa, and by this movement to render untenable all the fortifications established by the enemy during the past three months. He knew that this movement alone would bring about the evacuation of Drissa, and he hoped to attack them on the march. He left Vilna on the evening of the 16th, and reached Sventziani next morning. Hearing from Murat that the enemy had countered across the Dwina, and considering that this might indicate a general offensive movement on the part of the Russian First Army, he ordered the advance to stop; but later information pointing to Barclay's continued retreat, he directed the advance to proceed. Continuing his journey, Napoleon reached Glubokoye at midday on the 18th, and gave orders for the continued movement of his centre on Vitebsk. Eugene was to move on Kamen in the same direction.

Napoleon leaves Vilna

Barclay de Tolly, leaving Korf's corps at Drissa and Palen's at Disna, reached Polotzk on the 17th. On the 20th he marched on in two columns, which joined at Vitebsk on the 23rd. The corps left behind at Drissa

and Disna followed; but Wittgenstein was detached to form the right wing of the army in the neighbourhood of Drissa. The main French army also concentrated towards Vitebsk. Murat, with Ney's corps, three divisions of Davout's, and Nansouty's and Montbrun's cavalry, marched from Zamoshi on Disna, where Montbrun crossed the Dwina on the 22nd July, and continued his advance on Bieshenkovichy; while Oudinot, reaching Drissa the same day, moved on Polotzk. The Guard and Eugene's corps, marching by Glubokoye and Dokshitzi respectively, crossed the Ula at Bochyekovo, and reached Bieshenkovichy at the same time as Murat, on the 24th, and St Cyr's Bavarians marched to Ushach. Napoleon's headquarters were established at Bieshenkovichy[1] on the evening of the 24th July.

Barclay de Tolly in the first instance decided to give battle before Vitebsk. Hearing that the French were advancing on both banks of the Dwina, he, on the 24th July, detached Lieutenant-General Count Osterman-Tolstoi (who had succeeded Count Shuvalov) with the

[1] Napoleon established his headquarters in Count Boutenev's mansion. When staying at the mansion in 1892, the present writer saw there an old servant, over a hundred years of age, who had attended the Emperor, and well remembered how he gave a banquet to a glittering assemblage of his officers in the central hall of the house. Well might the old man say, like Béranger's peasant, "Children, through this village I saw him ride, followed by kings."

4th Infantry Corps and some cavalry to Ostrovno, to hold back the enemy and gain time. Seven versts from Vitebsk, Osterman met Nansouty's advanced troops, which were driven back by his cavalry and pursued as far as Ostrovno. Next morning Murat advanced, driving back Osterman's cavalry, and found the Russians in position astride the main road behind Ostrovno, their flanks protected by forest and marsh. The Russian cavalry were quickly overthrown by a charge of Polish lancers and hussars; but their infantry held their own and stopped the French advance until evening, when they fell back on the 3rd Infantry Division, posted in support at the village of Kakuviachin, eight versts from Ostrovno.

Murat advanced next morning with Nansouty's corps and Delzons' division, and came up with the **Action at Ostrovno** Russians at eight o'clock. The Russian front was covered by a deep ravine; their right flank rested on the Dwina, which was, however, fordable; their left was on a thick and marshy forest.

The French skirmishers advanced to the edge of the ravine, and engaged the Russians; while Delzons made dispositions to attack both their flanks and centre; some of Murat's cavalry crossed the Dwina to turn their right wing. The attack was rapidly carried out. The Russians repulsed the French on their left flank; but were driven back on the right. The Russian General

Konovnitzin reinforced his right with the whole of his reserve, which pressed the enemy's left and drove them across the ravine. The battle had, on the whole, favoured the Russians, when Murat charged a Russian column which had pursued the French across the ravine, while a further advance of French infantry against the left of their position forced them to retreat. Napoleon, who had arrived on the scene, directed the attack to continue, and Konovnitzin fell back in good order from position to position until evening, when he with Osterman rejoined the main army behind the River Luchosa. A new Russian advanced guard was pushed forward across that stream.

Napoleon bivouacked at Kakuviachin. Of the effect of his presence in action Ségur says: "The Emperor himself arrived. They (Murat and Eugene) hastened to receive him, and informed him in a few words of what had just been done, and what still remained undone. Napoleon instantly went to the highest point of ground and nearest to the enemy; and from that spot his comprehensive and ardent genius, levelling all the obstacles in its way, soon pierced both the shades of the forests and the depths of the mountains; he gave his orders without the slightest hesitation, and these same woods which had arrested the audacity of the two impetuous princes were traversed from one extremity to the other. In short, on that very evening, from the

Napoleon at Ostrovno

top of her double hill, Vitebsk might see our riflemen debouch into the plain by which it is surrounded."

Barclay de Tolly, in pursuance of his intention to give battle, had taken up a position behind the River Luchosa before Vitebsk. He had 80,000 men, and he hoped that Bagration would join him from Mohilev by way of Orsha. But on the night of the 26th July an aide-de-camp arrived with information from Bagration that he had been unable to get through by Mohilev, where Davout was concentrating his forces, and was doubtful of his ability to join the First Army even at Smolensk.

Operations at Vitebsk

Barclay de Tolly called a council of war; it was decided that there was now no object in fighting at Vitebsk, as even a successful action would be useless should Davout occupy Smolensk in the meantime. Further retreat was therefore imperative, although that operation would be difficult in the presence of the enemy. Accordingly Count Palen with the 3rd Cavalry Corps, reinforced to a strength of 14 battalions, 32 squadrons, and 2 regiments of Cossacks with 40 guns, was directed to hold the enemy on the road to Vitebsk.

With this object in view Count Palen occupied a position eight versts from Vitebsk, the front covered by a stream which fell into the Dwina, and the right flank on the Dwina. The left flank was quite open; and the extent of the position was too great for the strength available, the whole fourteen battalions only numbering 4000 men. These were disposed in two lines, with no reserve, and considerable intervals between battalions. The cavalry was drawn up on a small plain, where the stream fell into the Dwina, chequerwise in three or four lines, which led to considerable loss from the hostile artillery fire.

At dawn on the 27th July Napoleon sent his troops forward on the road to Vitebsk, the light cavalry in front followed by Broussier's division. The French soon came in contact with the Russian rearguard, and a sharp action ensued, during which the Emperor himself arrived on the scene. But it was not until Nansouty's cavalry and Delzons' infantry were all engaged that the Russians were forced to give way. At five o'clock in the afternoon Palen retired behind the Luchosa. The loss on either side during the three days' fighting amounted to some 3700 men.

Barclay de Tolly had in the first instance intended to remain on the Luchosa only until noon this day, but the resistance offered by his rearguard encouraged him in the hope of holding the enemy on that line until evening. Wishing to co-operate with Palen in delaying the French, he reinforced him from the main body and advanced his left wing to threaten the enemy's right flank.

Napoleon hoped to draw Barclay de Tolly into a decisive engagement. The French troops, tired with their long march, almost without bread and having for the most part nothing to eat but meat without salt, wished for a battle, hoping for something better. But the Russian general was already preparing to continue his retreat. At four o'clock in the morning the Russian army marched off in three columns towards Smolensk by way of Velizh, Poryechiye and Rudnya respectively. Count Palen's rearguard remained on the Luchosa until dawn on the 28th July. Large bivouac fires burning on the site of the encampment convinced Napoleon that his expectation of engaging the main Russian army would be realised.

But next day the French cavalry, taking up the pursuit, sustained a reverse from Palen's rearguard at Agaponovschina. **Forward Movement** The French troops being worn out for want of provisions and exhausted with the heat, and Napoleon no longer seeing the possibility of keeping the Russian armies separated, he decided to halt and rest his troops.

Napoleon's Central Army, acting against Barclay, was disposed as follows :—Headquarters and the Guard at Vitebsk. The Viceroy Eugene at Surazh, on the Dwina, formed the left wing of the army ; Murat's cavalry, with Ney in rear, was fronting Rudnya; three of Davout's divisions were behind Ney between Babinovichy and Vitebsk. St Cyr was at Bieshenkovichy. In the five weeks which had elapsed since the passage of the Niemen, Napoleon had succeeded only in occupying some useless territory, exhausted of supplies. The want of provisions caused widespread disorder, and the country was filled with bands of marauders who had left the army. There had been a vast loss of transport animals and of cavalry horses. The corps under the immediate leadership of Napoleon, detailed above, which had crossed the Niemen 200,000 strong, now numbered no more than 150,000 men; of the casualties not more than one-tenth had been killed, wounded, or made prisoners in action.

While he was at Vitebsk Napoleon heard of the Russian peace with Turkey, and of the treaty between Russia and Sweden.

Barclay de Tolly continued his retreat on Smolensk, where he concentrated his forces and encamped on the right bank of the Dnieper on the 1st August, on the roads leading to Poryechiye and Rudnya, at each of which places a rearguard was posted. His army was reinforced there by the reserve battalions and artillery companies under Winzingerode.

It is now time to direct attention to the operations against the Second Russian Army under Bagration, whom we left at Slutzk on the 13th July. The French cavalry had kept in touch with the Russians, and several actions took place in consequence, notably one in which the Ataman Platov met and repulsed the French cavalry at Romanovo.

Operations against Bagration

The troops under the King of Westphalia were moving, Vandamme from Nyesvizh on the line Minsk-Orsha; Poniatovski through Igumen on Mohilev; and Latour-Maubourg, having reached Glusk, followed towards Mohilev on the 26th July. Reynier's corps, as already related, had been sent back to Slonim to operate against Tormassov.

Davout continued his advance towards the Dnieper. He left Minsk on the 13th and reached Igumen on the 15th July, and entered Mohilev on the 20th.

In the meantime Bagration had assembled his whole army at Bobruisk on the 18th July, and next day received orders to effect a junction with the First Army by way of Mohilev and Orsha. But at the same time he had information of Davout's movement on Mohilev. Hoping to interrupt the enemy's concentration at that place, Bagration sent on a detachment under Raevski and followed next day with the remainder of his army. Raevski's cavalry fought an action with the French advanced troops between Stari Bikhov and Mohilev on the 21st July, in which 200 French were taken prisoners. Davout, determined to cover Mohilev, which was unfavourable for defence, took up an advanced position on the 22nd with 20,000 men at Saltanovka, where Bagration determined to attack him with a view to forcing a route by way of Mohilev and Orsha in accordance with his orders.

The Russians attacked at eight o'clock in the morning on

the 23rd and at first met with some slight success. But the French were in a strong position, their left resting on the Dnieper, and their front extended along a tributary of that river with their right thrown back. An attempt on their right flank failed, and the Russians were repulsed with a loss of 2500 men, the French losing an equal number.

Next day Davout strengthened the Saltanovka position in expectation of a further attack, but Bagration withdrew to Novi Bikhov and crossed the Dnieper at that place on the 26th July. Platov crossed the river higher up at Vorkolabov, and covered the Russian left flank, marching through Chaousi and Borki to Rudnya while Bagration retreated by Cherikov and Mstislavl to join Barclay de Tolly at Smolensk. The junction was effected on the 3rd August.

It was not until the 28th July that Davout moved from Mohilev. He feared to cross the Dnieper lest he should find himself between the two hostile armies, his strength being so greatly reduced that he only mustered 70,000 men. The King of Westphalia, whom Davout superseded, had left the army on the 16th July, and returned to his kingdom. Davout reached Dubrovna on the 2nd August. Thus at the end of July the French main army was extended between Surazh and Mohilev, where, however, Latour-Maubourg did not arrive until the 5th August.

While the events that have been narrated were taking place, operations had been in progress between Oudinot's corps and that of Wittgenstein, who, on the retreat of Barclay de Tolly's main army from Drissa to Polotzk, had been ordered to remain in the neighbourhood of Drissa to protect Riga and the country between Novgorod and the Dwina. In case of retreat being necessary he was to retire through Sebezh to Pskov, where magazines were established for the supply of his corps. Wittgenstein had 25,000 men and 100 guns.

Oudinot and Wittgenstein

When Napoleon advanced on Vitebsk, Oudinot's corps, supported later by St Cyr, was left to oppose Wittgenstein and threaten St Petersburg. He had some 20,000 men. He was on his left supported by Macdonald with 28,000 men, who occupied Jacobstadt on the 21st July, and established a garrison at Dinaburg a few days later. At the same time Oudinot moved up the Dwina towards Disna and Polotzk, which he had been directed to make his headquarters "if circumstances permitted." On the 26th he crossed the Dwina at Polotzk, with a view to taking the offensive against Wittgenstein, his instructions being to advance towards Sebezh and so cause the Russians to evacuate Drissa and Druya.

Wittgenstein had advanced towards Druya with the intention of crossing the Dwina at that place, when he heard of the advance of Macdonald and Oudinot on both his flanks. This determined him to fall back on Sebezh. On the 30th July his advanced guard came in contact with that of Oudinot at Yakubovo, where an indecisive action took place, at the end of which the French maintained their position. Wittgenstein renewed the attack at three o'clock the next morning, and after a hard-fought action drove Oudinot back two versts on Kliastitzi. There the French took up a second position, but they were defeated, their rear turned by the Russian cavalry and forced back to Boyarshchino behind the Drissa stream. Wittgenstein pursued, but his vanguard came into collision with the French in a strong position between two lakes in front of Boyarshchino and was driven back with heavy loss.

Oudinot again advanced as far as Golovshchitzi; there Wittgenstein, having heard of the action at Boyarshchino, had taken up a position with his right on the River Nishcha. He defeated the advancing French, and drove them back across the Drissa; Oudinot re-entered Polotzk on the 3rd August. Being reinforced by St Cyr on the 7th August, the French marshal again advanced but was met and defeated by Wittgenstein at Svolna on the 11th August, and once more fell back on Polotzk, where he arrived on the 16th.

In the meantime Macdonald had continued at Yakobstadt and Dinaburg, while the Prussian contingent of his corps laid siege to Riga.

On the extreme right Reynier and Schwarzenberg had been operating against Tormassov, and were at Slonim on the 3rd August. Napoleon directed Schwarzenberg, who commanded the whole forces of this flank, to march against Tormassov and Kamenski, and to follow them until they were destroyed. On the 12th August Schwarzenberg attacked the Russians at Gorodechna, and after an indecisive action in which Reynier's attack on the enemy's left flank failed, Tormassov retreated to Kobrin.

Movements of Schwarzenberg

It is clear that the Russian retirement to the Drissa camp was in contravention of all strategical principles. The two Russian armies which had been separated by Napoleon's advance were retiring on divergent lines instead of drawing nearer in order to effect a junction; while Drissa was on the flank of the main roads leading to the interior of the Empire. For this false move Barclay de Tolly was not entirely to blame, as has already been explained, and he rectified the error by moving to Vitebsk as soon as he found Drissa both strategically and tactically untenable. Had he lingered there, Napoleon would undoubtedly have closed in on him by his advance on Polotzk and cut off and destroyed his army. Who could suppose that a position that had taken months to prepare would be so soon evacuated; or instead of ordering his movement on Polotzk in order to destroy Barclay's army, Napoleon might otherwise have

Comments

adopted a more central line of advance and occupied Vitebsk before the Russians reached that place.

But the Emperor wrote on the 15th July that he "does not intend to attack the enemy either in their intrenched camp at Dinaburg or in their intrenched camp at Drissa; he intends to turn their positions, render them untenable, and attack the enemy on the march."

Arrived at Vitebsk, Barclay de Tolly intended to give battle, expecting the co-operation of Bagration, who had been ordered to march on Orsha. It was fortunate that the former heard that Bagration had been obliged to change the direction of his march in time to extricate his army and retire on Smolensk.

Bagration's retreat was boldly executed, and his offensive movement against Davout was not without effect in keeping that general on the right bank of the Dnieper.

CHAPTER VII

FROM THE DWINA TO THE DNIEPER

Napoleon at Vitebsk—Distribution of the French Forces—Russians assume the Offensive—Skirmish at Inkovo—French Dispositions—Russian Movements—Napoleon's Advance—Passage of the Dnieper—Cavalry Action at Krasnoi—Russian Dispositions—Comments

NAPOLEON remained at Vitebsk until the 13th August. But in the meantime the Russians assumed the initiative.

Napoleon at Vitebsk They were now concentrated at Smolensk to the number of 120,000 men. The French on the front Polotzk-Vitebsk-Mohilev were reduced to 229,000.

On the 6th August Barclay de Tolly called a council of war. The Tzar, the nation and the army were all demanding a cessation of the retreat which had already abandoned so much territory to the invaders. The Russian general knew that his forces were insufficient for decisive action. But it was decided to adopt the offensive.

While Barclay had been retreating to Smolensk, Napoleon had been employed in resting his army and seeing to supply. Many stragglers rejoined; the artillery parks and waggons, which had been left far in rear, arrived at Vitebsk ; the corps commanders collected seven days' provisions in the country. The Russian magazines seized in Surazh and Velizh served for the 4th Corps and the Guard. For the passage of the Dnieper and preservation of communications with Davout's troops, Napoleon ordered the construction of four bridges at Rasasna.

When the Russian armies retreated on Smolensk, the French were disposed as follows :—The Guard and one of Davout's divisions stood at Vitebsk, where Napoleon had his headquarters in the Governor-General's house. Two divisions of the same corps were at Pavlovichy, between Vitebsk and Babinovichy ; the 4th Corps, Eugene's, was at Velizh and Surazh ; Murat's cavalry reserve, Montbrun's and Grouchy's corps (with the exception of Doumerc's cuirassier division which was with Oudinot) at Rudnya, with Sebastiani's division as advanced guard at Inkovo ; Ney's corps in rear of the cavalry at Liozna. Davout's remaining two divisions were on the Dnieper between Babinovichy and Dubrovna ; the 8th (Westphalian) Corps under Junot was at Orsha; the 5th (Polish) Corps of Poniatovski at Mohilev ; Latour-Maubourg's Cavalry Corps and Dombrovski's Polish division were detached from Mohilev to observe Bobruisk and the Russian General Ertel's corps, which was at Mozyr. These troops, on the 3rd August, numbered 156,886 infantry and 36,722 cavalry, altogether 193,000 men, or

Distribution of the French Forces

excluding Latour-Maubourg's and Dombrovski's troops acting separately, the main strength of the French army for operations towards Smolensk was 182,608 men.

Napoleon intended, covered by the forests and marshes between the opposing forces, to execute a flank movement to his right, cross the Dnieper at Rasasna, seize Smolensk, and thus turning the Russian left, cut their line of retreat to Moscow and destroy them.

The Russian armies left Smolensk for their offensive movement in three columns on the 7th August, leaving only one regiment to garrison the city. The Second Army, 30,000 strong, passing through Smolensk on the right bank of the Dnieper, formed the left column along the bank of the river to the village of Katan, and the First Army, 70,000, marched in two columns, the left, under Dokhturov, moving by the Rudnya road on Prikaz Vidra; the right, under Tuchkov, by the Poryechiye road to Zhukovo, and afterwards to the left by Shchegolyeva on Kovalevskoye. Each column furnished its own advanced guard.

Russians assume the Offensive

A detachment of a division of infantry with some cavalry and fourteen guns, under General Olenin, had been posted at Krasnoi to observe the road from Orsha. On the right flank of the advancing army a detachment under Prince Shakhovski marched on Kasplya, and Krasnov's Cossacks on Kholm. Another detachment furnished from both armies, under Baron Rosen, preserved communication between Bagration and Dokhturov, marching on the village of Chaburi. Platov's advanced troops stayed that day at Zarubenka, so as not to expose the general advance of the Russian armies.

During the night Barclay de Tolly heard from Baron Winzingerode, who was with a detachment at Velizh, that the enemy was assembling in force at Poryechiye. This information was sufficient to cause further vacillation on the part of the Russian general, whose timidity was, perhaps, justified by the great forces and renown of his opponent. He concluded that Napoleon intended to move from Poryechiye on Smolensk and cut him off from Moscow; and he decided to abandon the offensive and turn his attention exclusively to the security of his right flank. He wrote to the Tzar: "Having a skilful and cunning opponent, able to take advantage of every circumstance, I find myself under the necessity of observing the strictest rules of caution." Accordingly on the 8th August a great part of the First Army (three infantry and one cavalry corps) was transferred to Lavrova and Stabna on the Poryechiye road; the remaining part (two infantry and two cavalry corps), under command of Dokhturov, was posted at Prikaz Vidra, whither the Second Army was also directed to march. In this situation, Barclay wrote to the Tzar, "both our armies will be only one march from one another; the road to Moscow and the whole region between the sources of the

Dwina and Dnieper will be covered, and supplies will be secured by the facility of transporting them from Velikia Luki, and Toropetz and Bieyloi." By the occupation of the road to Poryechiye he "would be able to strike the enemy's left flank with superior forces, to open communications with the Upper Dwina and cover Wittgenstein's left wing. Such a position has undoubted advantages and gives complete freedom of action according to circumstances."

The abandonment of the offensive by Barclay de Tolly pleased neither his staff nor the army in general. Bagration considered that there was more danger to be apprehended on the left than on the right flank of the Russian army. Displeasure manifested itself throughout the army, where it was thought that the indecision of the Commander-in-Chief deprived the army of the prospect of victory; some even accused him of treachery. The small successes which the Russian advanced troops had obtained in desultory actions had raised their spirits and inspired them with confidence.

On the 8th August the Ataman Platov attacked the French at Molevo Boloto near Inkovo with his Cossacks **Skirmish at** and some cavalry and infantry supports, **Inkovo** taking 300 prisoners and seizing Sebastiani's papers, from which it was found that the French were aware of the Russian concentration towards Rudnya. Again treachery was suspected, but it was discovered

FROM THE DWINA TO THE DNIEPER 85

that the information had been obtained through the letter of a Russian officer to his mother, in whose house near Rudnya Murat was quartered.

On the 9th August the Russians continued their flank movement; Dokhturov moved to Moshchinki, where headquarters were established; Platov retreated to Gavriki; the Second Army moved to Prikaz Vidra, its advanced guard, under Major-General Vasilchikov, standing at Volokova on Platov's left.

Napoleon, hearing of the skirmish at Molevo Boloto, took immediate measures to concentrate in order to oppose the expected Russian advance. He **French Dispositions** directed Ney and Murat to hold the enemy back on the Rudnya road; three divisions of Davout's from Vitebsk and the 4th (Eugene's) Corps were sent to join Murat and Ney at Liozna; Davout, Junot (Westphalians) and Poniatovski with his Poles and Latour-Maubourg's cavalry were to concentrate between Rasasna and Liubavichy. Thus 178,000 men could be collected in two days—or by the 10th August—on a front of thirty versts between Liozna and Liubavichy, or between Babinovichy and Dubrovna. Dombrovski with 6000 remained in Mohilev.

While the Russian First Army remained on the Poryechiye road, the Second Army marched from Prikaz Vidra to Smolensk on the 12th August on Bagration's initiative, the excuse given being the want of good water, which was a difficulty with both opposing armies owing to the prolonged summer heat. Bagration wished to **Russian** protect his left flank being turned by the **Movements** occupation of Smolensk. His advanced guard, under Vasilchikov, remained at Volokova; with a support of a grenadier division and eight squadrons of lancers under Prince Gorchakov at Debritza.

This movement took place just when Barclay was preparing to renew his advance on Rudnya. On the 14th August his army was disposed between Volokova and Lake Kasplya, with headquarters at Gavriki; he expected the French to attack on the 15th August, Napoleon's birthday. Two corps of Bagration's army again left Smolensk and marched to Katan.

Napoleon now saw that the Russian advance had ceased with the occupation of the Volokova position, and **Napoleon's** in order to cut them off from Moscow by the **Advance** occupation of Smolensk he executed a flank movement to the passages of the Dnieper at Rasasna and Khomino with the army under his immediate leadership, while the corps under Davout moved from Orsha and Mohilev towards Rasasna and Romanovo.

Napoleon left Vitebsk before daybreak on the 13th August and stopped for a time at a house in Babinovichy; resuming his journey on horseback, he arrived at Rasasna in the evening. Eye-witnesses described him as distinguished by the plainness of his attire in the midst of a glittering staff. At Rasasna he entered the house of a Jew, Hirsch Yudkin, but, finding it unfit for habitation, had his five-roomed tent pitched. He rode round to see his troops and afterwards had a long interview with Davout, who had just arrived. Later in the evening, bareheaded, at times clasping his hand to his head, buried in deep thought, he paced up and down a path in the forest. Close by is still shown a chasm into which numbers of corpses of the French were thrown during the retreat from Moscow. Here the waters of the Boristhenes, which the Romans had known only by their defeats, were passed by the legions of the great Emperor.

The troops, detailed, crossed the Dnieper at Rasasna and Khomino on the 13th and 14th August, joining the **Passage of the Dnieper** forces of Davout, Poniatovski and Junot, so that on the latter date Napoleon stood on the left bank of the Dnieper with 185,000 men: by a movement on Smolensk he hoped to cut the Russian communications with Moscow. Only Sebastiani's light cavalry division remained on the right bank of the river for the march to Smolensk.

At dawn Murat with the cavalry corps of Grouchy, Nansouty and Montbrun, 15,000 strong, reached Liadi, **Cavalry Action at Krasnoi** drove out a Russian detachment, and rode on to Krasnoi, where Neverovski had taken up a position with one of Bagration's divisions. The Russians fell back to Koritniya, holding off the

French cavalry, but suffering heavy losses during the retirement.

Barclay de Tolly heard of this action on the night of the 14th August. But he still did not know that Napoleon had made a change of front, had crossed the Dnieper and was turning his left flank, which he had thought secured by that river. The only movement **Russian Dispositions** made was to send Raevksi with his corps back to Smolensk, with orders to march to the support of Neverovski on the Krasnoi road. But he decided in consultation with Bagration that the latter should cross the Dnieper at Katan to oppose the enemy on the left bank, the First Army supporting him, following the French army and protecting the country between the Dnieper and Dwina. He wrote to the Tzar on the 15th: " Although the enemy's movement to the Dnieper and on the left bank of the river, by which he abandons almost the whole region between the Dwina and the Dnieper, gives cause for astonishment; as soon as I satisfy myself as to his real intentions, I shall not neglect to arrange operations according to actual circumstances, and I shall so dispose the army that it will always, while in a position to support the Second Army, at the same time hold the country between the Dwina and the Dnieper." But he was soon obliged to change his plan of operations, and to hurry all the troops back to Smolensk.

Raevski reached Smolensk at dawn on the 15th August, left by the Krasnoi road, and joined Neverovski at two o'clock in the afternoon in front of the city. Before nightfall the Cossacks were driven in by the advancing French, and soon the hostile masses were seen to occupy a position for the night on the Russian front. Raevski, seeing that he would be surrounded, decided to retire and take up a position to defend Smolensk itself.

In the phase of the operations between Vitebsk and Smolensk there were two movements of special interest
Comments —the Russian offensive advance, and Napoleon's great flank movement across the Dnieper to the south of Smolensk.

The Russian offensive was well conceived but badly executed. Vacillation and irresolution were evident in the Russian counsels; the ablest conceived plans will not command success unless carried through with resolution.

In advancing on Smolensk, Napoleon hoped to master the Russian communications with Moscow, as he had done in the case of the Austrians at Marengo in 1800. He was, in fact, carrying out a favourite strategical manœuvre, which was splendid in conception and might have been decisive in result. He knew that the Russians had advanced from Smolensk, and he arrived before that place twenty-four hours ahead of them. They had, however, thrown a small force behind the strong walls of the city, and it was not due to any fault either of conception or execution that Napoleon's plan failed. The place was sufficiently strong, as will be seen in the next chapter, to enable a small force to hold it until the main Russian army arrived.

CHAPTER VIII

THE BATTLE OF SMOLENSK

Smolensk—Raevski's defensive Measures—Napoleon arrives before Smolensk—French Dispositions—Russian Plans—Bagration's Retreat—Attack on Smolensk—Russian Retirement—Napoleon enters Smolensk—Barclay's Retreat continued—Action at Lubino—Comments—The Decision to advance on Moscow

Smolensk

THE town of Smolensk lies on both banks of the River Dnieper; its main portion is built on the left bank, which in the town itself descends rapidly to the river; the wide St Petersburg suburb is situated on the right bank, which commands the left. The town itself is surrounded by an ancient crenellated wall, built of stone and brick in the time of Godunov, having a circumference of more than five versts, a height of 25 to 40 feet, and a width of 10 to 18 feet. For flank defence thirty-six bastions had been built, but only seventeen of these remained intact in 1812. A pentagonal earthen bastion had been constructed by King Sigismund after the capture of the place by the Poles in 1611, on the western side of the town between the Krasnoi and Mstislavl suburbs. The exterior ditch of this citadel (known as the King's Bastion) was dry; the interior—

a wet ditch, crossed by a bridge. The ditch surrounding the town wall was not deep, and had been dug only to obtain the earth required for the glacis. Some emplacements had been made for guns behind the walls, and there was a covered way. Smolensk has three gates: the first, at the junction of the roads from Krasnoi, Mstislavl and Roslavl, is called the Malakhov; to its west lies the Mstislavl suburb; and to the east of this gate and of the Mstislavl road extend the Roslavl and Nikolskoye suburbs; the last communicates with the city through the Nikolskoye gate; farther, on the north-eastern side of the town by the river, lies the Rachenka suburb, through which passes the road through Shein Ostrog to Prudishchevo. Near these two villages are fords of the Dnieper—the one four and the other eight versts from Smolensk. The third entrance—the Dnieper gate—is turned towards the river. Besides these gates there are two passages through the walls: one to the left of the Dnieper gate, known as the Dnieper passage; the other, at the north-eastern corner near the river, the Rachenka passage. These were constructed on the occasion of the visit of the Empress Catherine II., for whose carriage the Dnieper and Malakhov gates were too narrow. An earthwork, constructed by the order of Peter the Great, covered the wooden bridge which communicated from the town to the right bank of the Dnieper. This work was under fire from the right bank of the river.

On the east and west the defence of Smolensk is strengthened by the Rachevka and Churilovka streams, flowing through deep ravines into the Dnieper near the Rachenka and Krasnoi suburbs. In the town itself three small streams run in similar deep ravines.

In expectation of the enemy's appearance, Raevski had disposed his troops as follows for the defence :—three **Raevski's Defensive Measures** regiments in the Krasnoi suburb and covered way to the right of the King's Bastion, with two guns commanding the approach. Three regiments and eight guns occupied the King's Bastion. Four regiments and twenty-four guns held the Mstislavl suburb. Two regiments and twenty-four guns were in the Roslavl suburb and in the cemetery in front. One regiment and four guns in the Nikolskoye suburb. Two regiments in reserve. Two regiments and four guns at the bridge over the Dnieper. Finally, twelve squadrons of cavalry were posted for observation on the left flank.

At eight o'clock in the morning of 16th August Ney's corps and Murat's cavalry arrived within cannon-shot of Smolensk. Ney's corps deployed against **Napoleon arrives before Smolensk** the Krasnoi and Mstislavl suburbs with their left flank on the Dnieper and their right on the Mstislavl road, while Grouchy's cavalry drove the Russian cavalry into the Nikolskoye suburb. Napoleon himself arrived at nine o'clock, when Davout's corps began to approach. Ney moved a body of his troops to attack, and himself led an assault on the King's Bastion. But the position was a strong one; reinforcements were hurrying into Smolensk, and the Russians held their own, Bagration arriving by midday, while Barclay de Tolly reached the place before nightfall, and took up a position on the high ground on the right bank of the Dnieper. The French during the day limited themselves to a cannonade of the suburbs and to feeble attacks, and at night encamped in a semicircle round the town. Napoleon had hoped that the Russians would come out and give battle in front of the town, and consequently the attack was not pressed. On the evening of the 16th August the French troops were disposed as follows:—On the

French Dispositions — left wing, opposite the Krasnoi suburb, three divisions of Ney; in the centre, opposite the Mstislavl and Nikolskoye suburbs, five of Davout's divisions; on the right, opposite Rachenka, Poniatovski's two divisions; and farther to the right, near the Dnieper, Murat's three cavalry corps. The Guard stood in reserve in the centre. Eugene's corps was still between Krasnoi and Koritniya, and Junot's had lost the way and did not arrive until evening.

The Russians generally considered that the time had now arrived to put an end to the advance of the French. But Barclay de Tolly with more reason saw the danger of opposing at this point a superior enemy who was in a position to threaten his line of communications with Moscow by crossing the Dnieper at **Russian Plans** Prudishchevo. He decided to continue the retreat along the Moscow road, covered by a corps of 20,000 men holding Smolensk under General Dokhturov, who relieved Raevski at dawn on the 17th August. Dokhturov posted a division in the Krasnoi and the King's Bastion; another in the centre to defend the Mstislavl and Roslavl suburbs; a third division formed the left wing in the Nikolskoye and Rachenka, in front of the left flank of which the cavalry was posted near the Dnieper; whilst a division was held in reserve near the Malakhov gate. The artillery was distributed in the King's Bastion, the terrace of the Malakhov gate, on the bastions and in the Mstislavl suburb. Two pontoon bridges were thrown across the Dnieper to provide additional communication with the right bank, where strong batteries were posted above and below Smolensk to enfilade the enemy in case they should attack the western or eastern side of the town.

Bagration began his retreat at four o'clock in the morning on the 17th August, and took up a position **Bagration's Retreat** behind the Kolodnya stream, eight versts from Smolensk, Barclay's army remaining in the vicinity of the city. Skirmishing in the suburbs of Smolensk began at daybreak, and at eight o'clock Dokhturov made a sortie from the town into the suburbs and drove out the enemy. Until three in the afternoon the action was limited to cannonade and musketry, and the French fire was not directed on the town. Napoleon still hoped that the Russians, having possession of Smolensk and being able to pass the Dnieper freely under cover of its strong walls, would cross over and give battle to protect the town.

Napoleon, about midday, receiving information from the right flank of his position of the movement of considerable Russian forces on the Moscow road, went to the village of Shein-ostrog and personally convinced himself of Bagration's retreat. He then proposed to cross the Dnieper above Smolensk and envelop the Russian left. But in order to carry out this project the whole army would have to ford the river, for if any attempts were made to construct bridges the Russians would oppose them at the selected points, or, passing through Smolensk, would assail the flank and rear of the French army; in any case the construction of bridges would take so much time that the Russians would be able to decline battle and retreat by the Moscow road. Napoleon, after considering these circumstances, sent some scouts to look for fords, but none were found. The only alternative was to take Smolensk.

The attack began at three o'clock in the afternoon, when the French cavalry overthrew the Russian dragoons and drove them headlong into the town through the

Malakhov gate, killing their general, Skalon. Poniatovski then attacked the Nikolskoye suburb and the

Attack on Smolensk Rachenka, with his right flank on the Dnieper, and established a battery of sixty guns on the bank of the river. The suburbs were fired in several places, and the Poles reached the wall of the town, attempted to storm, but were driven back with heavy loss. Ney in the meantime got possession of the Krasnoi suburb. Davout attacked and gained the Mstislavl and Roslavl suburbs after a stubborn fight, but the walls of the city proved an insuperable obstacle. Fierce assaults were concentrated against the Malakhov gate, but time after time the French were driven back. Finally towards evening the attacks ceased, and the assailants contented themselves with a cannonade which did much damage and fired the town in many places. Another assault at seven o'clock failed, and by nine the battle ceased. The French had lost some 6000 and the Russians 4000 men.

A fearful night succeeded the day. The Russians could no longer hold out amid the burning ruins which surrounded them, and Barclay de Tolly ordered the evacuation of the town. Dokhturov marched two hours before dawn, taking his artillery, after burning the bridges across the Dnieper.

Barclay's army assembled in position on both sides of the Poryechiye road, with the left flank on the village

G

of Krakhotkina, leaving a rearguard in the St Petersburg suburb to cover the retreat of the last defenders

Russian Retirement
of Smolensk. The town, which was nearly all burnt, was evacuated not only by the troops but by the inhabitants, so that when Napoleon entered it next morning by the Nikolskoye gate he

Napoleon enters Smolensk
found little besides a blackened heap of ruins. Ney sent some Wurtemberg and Portuguese battalions across the river to occupy the St Petersburg suburb, but the Russian rearguard, being reinforced, drove them back, and held the suburb throughout the day on the 18th August.

That morning Bagration continued his retreat by the Moscow road to Pneva Sloboda, near Solovyova, leaving a detachment under Prince Gorchakov to remain near Lubino until relieved by troops of the First Army.

Barclay de Tolly, having rested his troops during the day, marched in the evening, taking the route by Sushchovo and Prudishchiye with a view to joining the Moscow road at Solovyova, where it crossed the Dnieper.

Napoleon remained in inaction at Smolensk on the 18th August. He had no information as to the position of the enemy, and the fords of the Dnieper were unknown, in the absence of spies and of guides. With knowledge on these points he might yet be in a position to keep separate the armies of Barclay de Tolly and Bagration by an immediate passage of the river at the fords of Prudishchevo. At Smolensk the crossing of the Dnieper was delayed by the necessity for the construction of bridges, the permanent wooden bridge and two pontoon bridges having been destroyed.

Barclay de Tolly moved his troops in two columns, which were to reach Solovyova in two marches. The first, under Dokhturov, was to march by the Petersburg road to Stabna, and thence through Zikolino and Sushchovo to Prudishchiye, rest there and reach Pneva Sloboda next day. The second column, under Tuchkov 1st, accompanied by the Commander-in-Chief himself, would follow the Petersburg road only as far as Krakhotkina, and march by Polueva, Gorbunovo, Zhabino, and Kashayevo, and so by the Moscow road to Solovyova. A rearguard under General Korf was to follow this column. Platov's Cossacks were to form a line of detachments from Smolensk to Poryechiye, and as the columns approached Solovyova, he was to extend his left to the Dnieper and form a general rearguard. A special advanced guard, under General Tuchkov 3rd, was to move ahead of Tuchkov 1st's column through Gorbunovo on to the Moscow road.

Barclay's Retreat continued

This advanced guard, owing to the difficulty of the roads through forest and marsh, did not debouch on to the Moscow road until eight o'clock on the morning of the 19th August. Prince Gorchakov, commanding the detachment left by Bagration, had marched on to Solovyova without waiting to be relieved by troops of the First Army, leaving only three regiments of Cossacks to observe the Smolensk road. Tuchkov 3rd could not, therefore, march on, or he would leave open the point by which the column would debouch on to the Moscow road. He accordingly moved a short distance towards Smolensk, and at ten o'clock took up a position with his 3000 men behind the Kolodnya stream, with Karpov's Cossacks covering his left to the Dnieper. He had information that Junot was constructing bridges with a view to crossing the river at Prudishchevo, and that French troops were moving out from Smolensk to the Moscow road.

In the meantime a portion of one of Barclay de Tolly's corps had lost its way in the forest, and emerged at Gedeonovo in the morning when Ney, who had crossed the Dnieper by bridges constructed during the night, was forming up his corps in front of the Petersburg suburb, only 1500 yards distant.

Barclay de Tolly happened to appear at this point, and made arrangements for the troops to occupy the defensive position, to cover the retreat of the remaining corps which had lost their way to Gorbunovo. Thus, while the Russians had not yet effected their retreat, and had had to post detachments at two points to cover the movement,

Ney was in a position to attack and Junot was in a situation to advance and appear on the rear of the First Army. But Ney delayed his advance until after eight o'clock in the morning, giving the Russians (commanded by Prince Eugene of Wurtemberg) time to prepare the Gedeonovo position for defence. At length the French advanced, cut off a battalion, and forced back the Russians, who were only saved from destruction by timely reinforcements of cavalry, which covered their retreat to Gorbunovo.

Napoleon, informed that Ney had met with the enemy, ordered Davout to follow, and directed Junot to cross the Dnieper at Prudishchevo. The Guard and Prince Eugene remained in Smolensk, and Poniatovski's corps on the left side of the Dnieper, above Smolensk. Napoleon himself proceeded to the front, ordered Ney to advance along the Moscow road, and, although the cannonade was becoming more sustained, returned to Smolensk at above five o'clock, after giving orders to Murat and Junot to co-operate in the advance on Ney's right. He considered that the action was only an ordinary rearguard one, and, unaware that Barclay's army was retreating by a circuitous route and not by the Moscow road, had been unable to grasp the importance of Tuchkov 3rd's position behind the Kolodnya.

The action there began with Ney's attack soon after midday. But Tuchkov 3rd was reinforced by some 2000 men from the corps of Tuchkov 1st, and it was not until three o'clock that he was forced back behind the Stragan stream, where he had collected 8000 men by four o'clock, and the command devolved on General Ermolov. This position was of great importance, covering the retreat of Tuchkov 1st's columns when they debouched on to the Moscow road.

Action at Lubino

The Russians offered a stubborn resistance, but at nine o'clock in the evening they were forced to retire, with the loss of their brave leader, Tuchkov 3rd, who was wounded and captured when leading a final bayonet charge to cover the withdrawal of his wounded. Junot had crossed the Dnieper early in the action, but he remained immovable in a retired position, and failed to co-operate in the attack, notwithstanding Murat's personal and repeated requests. Had he marched to Lubino on the Moscow road in rear of Tuchkov 3rd's position he would have cut the line of retreat of the First Army and so attained the object for which he had been despatched across the Dnieper at Prudishchevo. This action was attended with considerable loss on either side, the Russian casualties numbering 5000. Since Napoleon crossed the Dnieper at Rasasna he had lost some 20,000 men, and his army now numbered under 160,000, compared with the 363,000 with which he had passed the Niemen between Kovno and Grodno.

On the 20th August the troops of Tuchkov 1st's column reached Solovyova, where they joined Dokhturov and crossed the Dnieper by three pontoon bridges during that day and the next. There were now only Korf's rearguard and Platov's detachment on the right bank. These crossed under cover of guns posted on the left bank, which kept off the pursuing enemy. The First Army marched on to Usviatye on the 21st and 22nd August; and the Second Army was disposed on its left flank.

Napoleon's last great manœuvre terminated at Smolensk. His first was the piercing of the Russian centre by the advance to Vilna; his next, the attempted destruction first of Bagration, and then of Barclay de Tolly by the advance to Glubokoye, towards Polotzk. He had now tried to bring the Russians to battle at Smolensk, and had failed. The reasons of his failure before Smolensk are to be found in a variety of causes. First, perhaps, in the differences between the two Russian commanders, which impeded co-operation between them, and as a consequence rendered it impossible for them to deliver battle. Barclay attempted to assume the offensive as has been related, but was prevented largely by the action of Bagration. The latter wished to make a stand at Smolensk; the former was for retreat.

Comments

Events show the error of the commonly accepted idea that the Russian plan of campaign had been thought out with a view to drawing the invaders into the interior and so destroying them. The establishment of the camp at

Drissa and the constant urging of the Tzar that the retreat should cease are alone sufficient to prove that such a plan had not entered the heads of responsible authorities.

It has already been remarked that Napoleon's change of front, which took him across the Dnieper and turned the Russian left, was one of the finest movements that he had executed. The causes of failure have also been generally indicated. Tactical failure appears to have been due in the first instance to a want of vigour in pressing home the attack on the city, and to inability to find the fords over the Dnieper at Prudishchevo in good time. Subsequently, Junot's inaction after crossing the river at that place admitted of the escape of Barclay when he might have been cut off on the Moscow road.

It appears to be worth considering whether Napoleon would have done better to turn the Russian right instead of their left in the advance on Smolensk. By marching by way of Poryechiye he would have avoided the double passage of the Dnieper at Rasasna and Smolensk, and on arrival before that place he would have been in possession of the higher part of the city on the right bank of the river. But such a movement in a direction where the enemy was awaiting him would have eliminated the element of secrecy essential to the success of his plan; and it would have involved the separation of his forces as he would have been manœuvring away from instead of towards Davout, who was approaching from Mohilev.

Napoleon had now to decide whether to advance farther or remain in Smolensk until the next year. He had already considered the matter at Vilna, but had arrived at no definite conclusion, although he had told Jomini that his intention was to advance as far as Smolensk, form winter quarters there for the army, and return to Vilna to establish his own headquarters. But this was on the understanding that he would have defeated the Russians in a good battle. For political purposes he had established his Foreign Minister, Maret, at Vilna.

The decision to advance on Moscow

Several new factors had appeared subsequent to the opening of the campaign, which had so far not come up to his expectations. The conclusion of peace between Russia and Turkey, setting free the army of Moldavia, and the treaty with Sweden, as has already been mentioned, imperilled the safety of the wings of his army. He had expected the Russian forces on either flank to conform to the movements of their main army, but they remained facing Schwarzenberg on one flank and St Cyr on the other. This unexpected obstinacy on the part of Tormassov had hindered the general rising of the Poles that had been anticipated in Volhynia, while Wittgenstein held his own on the other flank.

Difficulties of supply and transport, which, in view of the vast preparations that had been made, were unexpected, had been met with from the very beginning of the campaign; and if the troops had suffered so much in friendly Lithuania what was to be expected on the hostile soil of ancient Russia? This had resulted in great losses to the army, both from sickness and from straggling, which must be expected to increase.

"Strategical consumption," to use the expressive term of Clausewitz, had reduced the strength of the army, so that the vast preponderance with which Napoleon had opened the campaign no longer continued, and the wasting disease would become more evident as the army advanced into the interior. The Emperor had been disappointed in the expected battle, and the time and opportunity for strategical manœuvring had passed away.

Finally, the events of Smolensk, which left to the conqueror nothing but the smoking ruins of a deserted city, proved that Napoleon was now engaged in a national war against a people whose religious and patriotic sentiments were aroused to the point of fanaticism.

The time had arrived when these matters had to be considered in forming a decision whether to advance on Moscow in pursuit of the retreating enemy, or to be satisfied with the position on the Dnieper and establish himself at Smolensk for the coming winter. The advance into the interior would draw out his communications in an attenuated line, while the Russians could base themselves on the whole extent of their vast Empire. It could surely be perceived that, failing the conclusion of peace at Moscow, the enterprise must fail.

On the other hand, to halt in cantonments on the Dnieper appeared impossible while the enemy had not been defeated in a decisive battle. Supplies could not be ensured for a large army which it would be necessary to keep concentrated in the face of the undefeated enemy. The harvest of 1811 was a bad one; that of 1812 had been spoilt by the ravages of war and the withdrawal of the population. The base might have been changed by a retirement by way of Lutzk and Brest, which would have swept Tormassov aside and ensured supplies that were unattainable in ravaged Lithuania. But political considerations rendered a retrograde movement unthinkable. Even a halt on the Dnieper in existing circumstances would perhaps appear tantamount to failure in the eyes of Europe, which, subjugated but not pacified, was hostile at heart, and stood at gaze on the long line of communications with France.

It appeared then that the only course was to continue the advance in the hope of fighting a decisive battle and dictating terms of peace in the ancient capital of the Tzars. And who, without the wisdom that comes after the event, can say that Napoleon's decision to take this course was not a wise one? It was at any rate the only one that conformed with the character of the great Emperor whose ambition could brook no restraint.

CHAPTER IX

THE ADVANCE TO BORODINO

Russian Desire for Battle—French Pursuit—Napoleon leaves Smolensk—Measures in Rear—Russian Retreat continued—Kutuzov assumes Command—Action at Shivardino—Position of Borodino—Occupation of the Position—The Opposing Forces—French Dispositions—Napoleon's Orders

Russian Desire for Battle

THE Russians were now more anxious than ever to fight a decisive battle, and on the retreat from Smolensk their object was to find a position favourable for a defensive action. For this purpose staff officers were despatched on the road to Moscow, and two positions were found, one at Usvyatiye, behind the Uzha stream, and another at Tzarevo Zaimishchiye, about half-way to the Russian capital. The position at the former place being considered most favourable was taken up for defence. But when the French advance developed, weaknesses were discovered on both flanks, and the Russians withdrew to Dorogobuzh on the night of the 23rd-24th August.

Meanwhile Murat, followed by Davout and Ney, reached Pneva Sloboda on the 22nd, and crossed the Dnieper, the cavalry fording the river, the infantry by two

THE ADVANCE TO BORODINO

pontoon bridges; Junot followed. The heat was oppressive; troops, carts and flocks which followed the army moved in thick clouds of dust. Eugene's corps marched by Pomogailovo and thence by the Dukhovshchina-Dorogobuzh road, and on the 25th reached Zaseliye, where a junction was effected with Grouchy who had marched by Dukhovshchina. Poniatovski marched by Byelkino, following the course of the Dnieper at a distance of some versts from the main road. Latour-Maubourg marched on Mstislavl and thence to Yelnya where he was to arrive on the 28th.

French Pursuit

Napoleon, hearing that the Russians had taken up a position before Dorogobuzh, and hoping for a general engagement, sent his Guard forward on the 24th August, and left Smolensk that night. He had now about 155,000 men, exclusive of a garrison of 4500 left in Smolensk, where there were also some 6000 wounded. Such supplies as were found were despatched after the troops. In the course of a few weeks considerable magazines of flour and other provisions were established.

Napoleon leaves Smolensk

Meanwhile Napoleon had not neglected the flanks and rear of his army, to which he paid special attention now that he had advanced so far into hostile territory and, as he hoped, was about to complete the subjugation of the enemy by a decisive victory and the occupation of the ancient capital.

Measures in Rear

Marshal Victor, who was in Prussia with the 9th Corps, was directed to march by Kovno and Vilna to Smolensk. The detachments on the line of communications at those places and at Minsk, Mohilev and Vitebsk were placed under him. The Emperor wrote to Schwarzenberg: "You will try to reach Kiev while we go to Moscow." St Cyr, who had succeeded Oudinot, was directed to hold back Wittgenstein, and Macdonald to lay siege to Riga. The siege park was ordered up from Tilsit to the Dwina. After obtaining possession of Riga Macdonald's corps was "to take part in the general operations, and then Macdonald and St Cyr can threaten St Petersburg while we are in Moscow. Should St Cyr be defeated, Victor will move to the assistance of the troops operating on the Dwina. But the chief object of his army is to form a reserve for the Moscow army. In case of interruption of the communications between Smolensk and my headquarters, they must at once be reopened; it may be necessary for the Duke of Belluno (Victor) to march towards us. Perhaps I shall not find peace where I am going to seek it. But in that case, having behind me a strong reserve, I shall be in no danger and I need not accelerate my retreat." Augereau's corps was to occupy the country between the Vistula and the Niemen. Some of the Cohorts of the National Guard were moved to the Rhine and the Elbe. The conscription for 1813 was ordered. Thus the great Emperor made provision for everything, as Napier says, "with such a military providence, with such a vigilance, so disposing his reserves, so guarding his flanks, so guiding his masses, that while constantly victorious in front no post was lost in his rear, no convoy failed, no courier was stopped, not even a letter was missing: the communication with his capital was as regular and certain as if that immense march had been but a summer excursion of pleasure!"

But again Napoleon was disappointed in his expectation that the Russians would stand for battle. They **Russian Retreat continued** continued their retreat, the First Army to Viazma and the Second Army to Bikova, where they arrived on the 27th August. The same day their rearguard was attacked by Murat at Ribki on the River Osma, where it held out for seven hours until evening, when it retreated. On the 28th the Russians retreated to Fyoderovskoye and next day reached Tzarevo-Zaimishchiye, where they took up a position and where Barclay de Tolly intended to fight a battle. Their rearguard was engaged throughout the retreat, during which the Cossacks and horse-batteries were especially effective in delaying the enemy. The French occupied Viazma the same day, finding much of it burnt by the inhabitants, who had deserted the town and followed the troops.

Barclay de Tolly was now succeeded in command by

Kutuzov, an event which was not without effect on the nation and the army. Although Barclay was the more able commander of the two, the continual retreats and the abandonment of Smolensk, the holy city on the confines of Old Russia had lost him the confidence of the troops and of the people. Kutuzov, a Russian of the Russians, a lieutenant of Suvarov, had indeed been defeated at Austerlitz. But he was ready to give battle to the invaders, and he arrived at the psychological moment. Conditions were more favourable to him than they had been at any period of the campaign. The long marches, the bloody combats, the difficulty of obtaining provisions and forage, the extension of the line of communications had sapped the enemy's strength. The news of the battle of Salamanca had perhaps affected their *moral*. The conclusion of a treaty with Sweden had strengthened the Russian position; peace with Turkey had set free the Danubian army under Chichagov to co-operate against the French line of communications. As they retreated, the Russians gained in strength, and exhausted the resources of the country on the track that must be followed by the invaders. These causes tended to the equalisation of the forces in point of numbers.

Kutuzov assumes Command

Kutuzov, accompanied by Bennigsen, his Chief-of-the-Staff, reached the army at Tzarevo-Zaimishchiye on the 29th August. The new Commander-in-Chief decided to continue the retreat, in order to give time for filling up the ranks of the army now reduced to 95,000 men, but shortly reinforced by over 15,000 under Miloradovich, and by a considerable militia in the shape of untrained peasants who joined the army with cries of, " It is the will of God ! "

But although Kutuzov retreated, he had determined to give battle in accordance with the demand of the nation and the army. His arrival raised the *moral* of the troops in the highest degree, and they prepared for the coming struggle with full confidence in themselves, in their leader, and in the justice of their cause.

One of the new Commander-in-Chief's first acts was to inform Tormassov and Admiral Chichagov of his intention to fight a battle, and to tell them that, in view of the enemy having penetrated to the heart of Russia, their rôle no longer lay in the defence of remote Polish provinces, but in the distraction of the hostile forces massed against the main Russian army. He accordingly directed Tormassov to act against the right wing of Napoleon's Grand Army, while Chichagov, with the troops coming from Moldavia, would carry out the duties hitherto performed by Tormassov.

On the 31st August the Russian army left the position at Tzarevo-Zaimishchiye, passed through Gzhatsk and reached Ivashkovo, where Miloradovich joined with his 15,000 men. Their rearguard under Konovnitzin made a stand at Gzhatsk, but was driven out by Murat and Ney.

Napoleon reached Gzhatsk on the 1st September, and there heard of the arrival of the new Russian Commander-in-Chief, and of his intention to give battle. He accordingly stopped the advance in order to rest and organise his troops for the approaching conflict. Murat halted a short distance beyond the town. Ney and Davout were disposed round Gzhatsk, where the Guard was quartered. Eugene was at Pavlovo on the left and Poniatovski at Budayevo on the right front. Junot was coming on in rear. On the 4th September Murat and Davout were ordered forward to Gridnevo, the army conforming to their movements. There the Russian rearguard was met with, but not forced to retire until nightfall, when they fell back to Kolotzkoi Monastir. This position was attacked next day, and the Russians forced to retire by the advance of Eugene's corps on their right flank. They retreated to their main army, which had taken up a position about Borodino.

The advanced guard under Murat, followed by the Grand Army, crossed the Kalocha at Fomkino and Valueva, and turned to the right to Shivardino, where a Russian detachment under Prince Gorchakov stood on the heights in front of their main position, protected by a strong redoubt.

Napoleon sent three of Davout's divisions and Murat's

cavalry reserve against this post, and directed Poniatovski to turn it by advancing along the old Smolensk road. A fierce and bloody fight ensued, which continued until ten o'clock at night, when Shivardino finally remained in the hands of the French. This battle cost the Russians some 6000 and the French 4000 men. The Emperor's tent was pitched in the midst of his Guard at Valueva, on the left of the road to Moscow. In the afternoon he reconnoitred the enemy's position, but although he was active in a general way, Napoleon no longer displayed the activity of Austerlitz and Jena ; nor did he appear to possess that confidence in his fortune which had so often led him to victory.

Action at Shivardino

The position of Borodino extended from the village of Utitza on the old Smolensk road on the left to the Moscow (properly Moskva) River on the right. The right wing was covered by the River Kalocha, which in its upper portion flows through a marshy valley, parallel to the new Smolensk road which it crosses at the village of Borodino. Below that point, until its junction with the Moskva, the Kalocha runs through a deep ravine with precipitous sides, the right bank commanding the left, and in many places fifteen feet high. This right wing was the strongest portion of the position. Near Borodino three streams fall into the Kalocha : on the right, opposite the village, the Stonetz, between which and the Kalocha extends a narrow spur

Position of Borodino

with a lofty hillock at the village of Gorki ; above Borodino the Voina, flowing sluggishly through a marshy valley, joins the Kalocha on the left bank ; Borodino stands on the height which lies between the streams. Higher still—the Semyonovka flows out of the forest on the old Smolensk road to join the Kalocha on its right bank ; its banks are almost level in the upper part, but steep in the lower reaches. Between the Semyonovka, the Kalocha, and the Stonetz the high ground commands the surrounding country. On the summit is situated the spot known as Raevski's battery. From the village of Semyonovskaya to its mouth the right bank of the Semyonovka commands the left ; above Semyonovskaya the left bank is the higher.

Owing to the heat of the summer of 1812 these streams were all practically dry, and there was little water in the Kalocha. To the left of Semyonovskaya as far as the fields of the village of Utitza extended a bush-grown plain. The fields were surrounded on three sides by deep forests, traversed by the old Smolensk road. There is a considerable eminence close to the road in the forest behind Utitza.

From the Kamenka stream, a dry tributary of the Semyonovka marking the prolongation of the Russian front, the ground rises gradually in the direction of Fomkino, and of the line of the French advance. There are three knolls near Shivardino.

The Kalocha covered the right wing of the position only as far as Gorki; from that point the Russian line passed through Semyonovskaya and Utitza.

It will be understood, then, that the right flank and right wing of the Russian position was rendered strong by natural features. The centre and especially the left were weak, that flank resting on no natural obstacle and being liable to envelopment by a turning movement along the old Smolensk road.

The position was strengthened by earthworks. Two batteries, of three and nine guns respectively, were constructed—the one on the knoll just in front of Gorki, the other 200 yards farther down the road towards Borodino. The wooden bridge over the Kalocha was left standing and Borodino was prepared for defence. In the centre a large earthwork was made, with embrasures for ten guns; but the works generally were not as complete as they might have been, through a deficiency of entrenching tools, while the ground was difficult, being covered with stones. Farther to the left, in front of Semyonovskaya were three batteries, known as the Bagration redoubts.

Besides the works that have been enumerated, the wood on the left flank of the position was prepared for defence. The Moscow and Smolensk militia, numbering 10,000 men, being badly armed and trained, was employed in carrying the wounded and on baggage-guard.

The right and centre of the position were occupied by the First Army under Barclay de Tolly; the left, by the Second Army under Prince Bagration. The 2nd and 4th Infantry Corps under Miloradovich formed the right wing, covered by the Kalocha, extending from a point 800 yards from the Moskva River to the Stonetz stream behind Gorki. The 2nd Cavalry Corps stood in rear of the left of this wing; the 1st Cavalry Corps was considerably thrown back on the right rear, towards Uspenskoye, and Platov's Cossacks were formed upon its left. The 6th Infantry Corps, supported by the 3rd Cavalry Corps, under Dokhturov, occupied the high ground across the Stonetz, south of Gorki, extending to Raevski's battery.

Occupation of the Position

Of the Second Army the 7th Infantry Corps, with the 4th Cavalry Corps in rear, occupied the space between Raevski's battery and Semyonovskaya; and Count Vorontzov's division—the Bagration redoubts. The rifle regiments were distributed along the front with the exception of four regiments which occupied the bushes on the Kamenka stream and to the left in the direction of the old Smolensk road, and two which stood in a grove behind the right wing between the 2nd Infantry and 1st Cavalry Corps. Five Cossack regiments observed the lower Kalocha to its junction with the Moskva, and six, the left about Utitza, where Tuchkov's infantry corps was posted. The Bagration redoubts were occupied by guns and infantry; the others were defended only by guns. The infantry were not all covered by breastworks as had been intended.

The general reserve, consisting of the 3rd and 5th Infantry Corps and the 1st Cuirassier Division, was posted behind the village of Kniazkovo; the main artillery reserve of twenty-six companies and batteries,[1] behind Psarevo. The Second Army had its own reserve, consisting of Prince Charles of Mecklenburg's grenadier division, behind Semyonovskaya, subsequently reinforced by the Shivardino garrison and five companies of horse artillery sent from the general reserve. The headquarters were at Tatarinovo.

In all the Russians had 120,800 men, consisting of 72,000 infantry, 17,500 cavalry, 14,300 artillery and pioneers, 7000 Cossacks and 10,000 militia, and 640 guns. Napoleon's army numbered 130,000 men, of which 86,000 were infantry, 28,000 cavalry, 16,000 artillery and pioneers, and 587 guns, The opposing forces cannot be compared according to their numerical strength alone. The French army consisted of men inured to war; the weakly had been eliminated by the vicissitudes of the campaign which had resulted in the survival of the fittest. But the army

The Opposing Forces

[1] Those of the Guards were called batteries; they had eight guns.

suffered from want of provisions. The cavalry horses were mostly worn out and in bad condition, while the French guns were greatly inferior in calibre to those of the Russians. The Russian army comprised 15,000 ill-trained recruits, and 10,000 militia, many of whom were armed only with pikes.

It will be seen that as the right flank of the position was well protected by natural features, it might have been more lightly occupied, and it would perhaps have been sufficient to have observed that flank or held it lightly, and so set free a larger number for the general reserve, and for the exposed flank on the left, which was insufficiently held.

During the 6th Napoleon reconnoitred the Russian position. This was quite clear until their left was reached, where its limit could not be perceived as it was hidden by the forests about Utitza. In the evening he issued his orders for the battle, after posting Poniatovski in the forest on the right flank of the army near the Yelnya road. It is said that Davout urged a wide turning movement round the Russian left, to avoid a direct attack on the redoubts on that flank; but the Emperor considered this too dangerous, as it would divide his forces in the presence of the enemy.

<small>French Dispositions</small>

Davout was in position to the right front of Shivardino with the divisions of Friant, Dessaix and Compans;

the cavalry of Nansouty, Montbrun and Latour-Maubourg were in his rear. Ney stood between Shivardino and Alexinki; Junot behind him, and the Young and Old Guards in rear of him again; Morand was on Ney's left front, his left on the Kalocha, behind which stood Grouchy's cavalry; Morand and Grouchy were under Prince Eugene, whose divisions under Gerard, Broussier and Delzons stood in that order from right to left behind the Kalocha and the Voina stream, with the Italian Guard in the rear. The extreme left, beyond the Voina was watched by Ornano's cavalry, between Bezzubovo and Loginovo.

The orders issued directed two new batteries of twenty-four guns, constructed during the night on the plain **Napoleon's** occupied by Davout, to open fire on the two **Orders** opposing hostile batteries. At the same time the chief of artillery of the 1st Corps with thirty guns of Compans and all the howitzers of Dessaix's and Friand's divisions, was to move forward and shell the enemy's right battery at Semyonovskaya, against which the fire of sixty-two guns would be concentrated. Forty guns of the 3rd Corps were to open on the left fortification, and the howitzers of the Guard were to be in readiness to act according to circumstances.

During this artillery fire Poniatovski was to advance by the old Smolensk road, attack Utitza, and turn the enemy's position.

Compans was to move through the forest and attack the left redoubt.

Subsequent orders would be issued according to the enemy's movements.

The cannonade on the left flank would begin as soon as that on the right was heard. The skirmishers of Morand's division, and of Prince Eugene's divisions were to open a heavy fire when they saw the beginning of the right attack. The Prince was to occupy Borodino, cross the Kalocha by three bridges which he had been ordered to construct during the night, and conform to the movement of Morand's and Gerard's divisions, which were to attack the entrenchment of Gorki, and were placed under his orders.

These orders were to be carried out with order and method, keeping troops in reserve as far as possible.

In instructions issued to Davout by the Chief-of-the-Staff we read :

"The Emperor wishes that to-morrow the 7th at five o'clock in the morning Compans' division be drawn up by brigades in front of the Shivardino redoubt, having thirty guns in front of it. Dessaix's division will be disposed in the same manner between the redoubt and the forest with its fourteen guns on its left. Friand's division will be drawn up in line with the redoubt.

"Ney is directed to take the 8th Corps under his command. He will place three divisions of the 3rd Corps behind the Shivardino redoubt, drawn up in brigades with their guns on their left. The Imperial Guard will be drawn up on the left rear of the redoubt—the Young Guard in front of the Old Guard and artillery of the Guard; the artillery of the Guard disposed on the left flank.

"Murat's Cavalry, consisting of the 1st, 2nd, and 4th Reserve Cavalry Corps will be drawn up in order of battle by squadrons (en bataille par escadrons) to the right of the redoubt.

"All the troops will occupy their appointed stations by five o'clock."

To his troops Napoleon issued the following proclamation :—

"Soldiers! This is the battle which you have so much wished for. Victory depends on you. It is indispensable for us; it will ensure us all that is needful, comfortable quarters and a speedy return to the Fatherland. Do as you have done at Austerlitz, Friedland, Vitebsk, and Smolensk. Let remotest posterity recall with pride your deeds of valour on this day. Let it be said of each of you—He was at the great battle under the walls of Moscow!"

CHAPTER X

THE BATTLE OF BORODINO

Napoleon at Shivardino—Attack on the Russian Left—Eugene takes Borodino—Renewed Attack on Russian Left—Ney assaults the Left—Russians retake the Redoubts—Poniatovski's Advance—The Battle at Semyonovskaya—French Capture the Left Redoubts—Murat's Cavalry Charge—Capture of Semyonovskaya—Poniatovski at Utitza—The Battle in the Centre—Reinforcement of the Russian Left—Uvarov's Cavalry Charge—Renewed Attack on the Centre—Capture of Raevski's Battery—The Battle ends—Russian Position—Comments

NAPOLEON mounted his horse at half-past five in the morning of the 7th September, and rode to the Shivardino redoubt. He had slept little during the night, owing to the excitement of the impending battle, while his health was not good and he was suffering from a severe cold which almost deprived him of his voice. He remained nearly all day on the high ground in front of the redoubt, about a mile from the Russian first line; the Guard were drawn up round him. Here he paced up and down, stopping at times to issue orders.

Napoleon at Shivardino

Kutuzov had at the same time taken up his position at Gorki, where he remained until the end of the battle, at a considerable distance from the decisive flank.

The French batteries opened fire with 102 guns at six o'clock, but finding the range too great, they were moved forward, and reopened at about 1600 paces. This was followed by the opening of artillery fire in the centre and by Prince Eugene's guns against Borodino. The Russians replied from their batteries and redoubts. Under cover of the artillery fire Davout's two divisions moved to the attack—Compans on the right and Dessaix on the left. On emerging from the forest, the former came under fire from the redoubts and were driven back into cover, but at length they rushed to assault the left earthwork. At this moment Compans fell severely wounded, and his troops wavered, but Davout, seeing their hesitation, rode forward, led the attack and the redoubt was taken. Bagration had sent up reinforcements from the second line; these drove the French out again, and their discomfiture was completed by a charge of two regiments of Russian hussars and dragoons, who captured twelve guns, but were forced to abandon them and retire by two brigades of French light cavalry. During this struggle Dessaix was severely wounded, and Marshal Davout had his horse killed and received a severe contusion, but remained at his post.

Attack on the Russian Left

While this fight was in progress, Prince Eugene had attacked and occupied Borodino with Delzons' division, which drove out the Russians, who were pursued across the bridge over the Kalocha by a French regiment, which followed them to the vicinity of Gorki. There were in turn attacked by superior forces in front and flank, and forced back to Borodino with heavy loss. The Russians then destroyed the bridge over the Kalocha, while Prince Eugene contented himself at that point with holding Borodino. Delzons' division and the Bavarian cavalry stood behind the village; to the left was a strong battery firing on the Gorki heights and Raevski's battery; and farther to the left, in front of the village of Bezzubovo, Ornano's light cavalry stood upon the plain. Eugene's remaining troops (Gerard's and Broussier's divisions, the Italian Guard and Grouchy's cavalry) moved to the right towards the bridges which had been constructed across the Kalocha above Borodino, and crossed under cover of Morand's riflemen, who were engaged with the Russian skirmishers at the foot of Raevski's hill.

Eugene takes Borodino

Napoleon, hearing of the loss of general officers in the right attack, had sent Rapp to succeed Compans; but Rapp was soon wounded. The Emperor now, at seven o'clock, directed Ney to co-operate in Davout's attack, while Junot's corps was moved up to the left of Shivardino, and Murat's cavalry advanced to support.

Renewed Attack on Russian Left

Bagration, observing Ney's advance, took measures to oppose the enemy with reinforcements of both infantry and artillery, including all his reserve batteries, as well as one of Tuchkov's divisions, and sent to Barclay de Tolly for reinforcements. The latter despatched his 2nd Infantry Corps, in addition to some regiments of Guards from his reserve, grenadier battalions, and artillery, a measure which occupied a couple of hours, while Davout and Ney were already preparing to renew the assault.

It was eight o'clock. The fire at the redoubts had not ceased for a moment when Ney attacked Bagration's troops. He was met by a murderous fire of shot and musketry, but continued to advance. Ney himself at the head of a portion of his corps captured the left redoubt; others of Ledru's division seized the right one. Only then did the attackers perceive the third work, which was behind the others, and drove the Russian grenadiers out of it. A hand-to-hand fight ensued in which Count Vorontzov was severely wounded by a bayonet thrust, and the combat ceased only with the annihilation of his division.

Ney assaults the Left

At nine o'clock Bagration sent forward his reinforcements, referred to above, as well as a large force of cavalry and some horse artillery; while at the same time some light cavalry were despatched to assist Davout and Ney. No sooner did the Russian infantry move forward to retake the lost redoubts, than Murat sent his Wurtemberg horse against them, but

Russians retake the Redoubts

these were overthrown by a charge of Russian cuirassiers, which pursued them, entered the entrenchments, and drove out the French infantry. Murat himself only escaped being taken prisoner by dismounting and taking refuge in the left redoubt, occupied by a Wurtemberg battalion. The Russian cuirassiers were at length driven back by a regiment of Polish lancers.

About ten o'clock, after a renewed and desperate struggle, in which Prince Gorchakov and Neverovski were wounded, Ney's troops again obtained possession of the redoubts. But at this moment the reinforcements sent by Barclay de Tolly to reinforce the left wing were approaching the Semyonovskaya heights. They charged with the bayonet, and once more drove the French out of the field works.

Meanwhile Poniatovski had advanced along the old Smolensk road, and had gained possession of Utitza; his corps numbered only 10,000 men, and he could advance no farther against the Russian flank in the face of superior forces.

Poniatovski's Advance

Already at nine o'clock Napoleon, being informed that Ney's troops had captured the Semyonovskaya works, and thinking that he did not require the co-operation of the Westphalian corps, ordered Junot to move into the interval between Davout and Poniatovski, to combine the two attacks. News then came of Ney's repulse, but it was some

The Battle at Semyonovskaya

time before Napoleon decided what to do, and at length he sent Friand's division to reinforce him; it was eleven o'clock before Friand moved forward.

The French had now some 26,000 men attacking the Semyonovskaya entrenchments, where 18,000 Russians opposed them. There were numerous batteries on either side, whose fire was incessant. It was during this period that Bagration fell mortally wounded. Dokhturov succeeded to the command of the Second Army, while Konovnitzin commanded the troops at the redoubts. At about eleven o'clock the French again assaulted the earthworks, once more obtained possession of them, and the guns. But they did not hold them long, for they were soon driven out and forced back into the forest by a desperate bayonet charge of Borozdin's grenadiers.

At eleven-thirty a renewed attack drove the Russians out again, and the French now finally gained possession of the Semyonovskaya redoubts, the Russians retiring behind the watercourse, where Konovnitzin reorganised the remainder of the troops under cover of strong batteries.

<small>French capture the Left Redoubts</small>

Ney now attacked the village, but was repulsed; whereupon Murat, having conferred with him, decided to intervene in the battle with a great mass of cavalry. These were divided into two parts, to attack the Russians on either side of Semyonovskaya. To cover this attack, Ney and Davout

<small>Murat's Cavalry Charge</small>

established batteries along the margin of the watercourse. Nansouty, crossing with St Germain's cuirassiers and Bruyere's light cavalry division, above Semyonovskaya village, was met by a heavy fire from the Russian batteries. At the same time two regiments of Russian guards on the left wing formed six squares, and repelled the attack with their fire; two more charges met with the same result, and then one of the guards regiments charged in their turn with the bayonet, while the Russian guns played upon the cuirassiers until their fire was masked; and Nansouty's cavalry was driven back with heavy loss.

Latour-Maubourg had crossed the watercourse below the village with his two cavalry divisions, but the difficulty of the passage delayed him and he came into action later than Nansouty. Charging on the right and rear of the Russian infantry, this cavalry met with more success, but they also were forced to retire.

During this cavalry action Friand renewed the attack on the ruins of Semyonovskaya, of which he obtained possession, and his troops maintained themselves on the right bank of the watercourse, obliging the Russians to retire a cannon-shot from the ravine.

Capture of Semyonovskaya

On occupying Semyonovskaya, Ney established strong batteries which opened fire from the front against the Russian left wing and on the flank of their troops in the centre of their position. The Russian left wing was completely disorganised. Barclay de Tolly wrote: "The Second Army, in the absence of Prince Bagration and many generals wounded, was driven back in the greatest confusion; all the fortifications and portions of the batteries were in the hands of the enemy. The 26th Division alone still maintained its position about the heights in front of the centre."

Fortunately for the Russians, the thick dust which had risen from the cavalry attacks and the smoke of the guns to the number of about 700 concentrated around Semyonovskaya, prevented the enemy from observing the broken and weakened state of the Russian left.

The French generals did not consider that they had sufficient strength to confirm the successes they had gained, in view of their great losses. They stood at Semyonovskaya, and sent to Napoleon for reinforcements. But the Emperor feared to use up his only reserve—the 19,000 men of the Old and Young Guard—and after some hesitation he sent a division of the Young Guard, with orders not to advance beyond the Kamenka.

In the meantime in the centre and on the Old Smolensk road the battle was being fought with varying fortune. **Poniatovski at Utitza** Poniatovski had started at five o'clock, but his movements were so slow that his leading division did not reach the road until eight. His troops occupied the village of Utitza, but stopped beyond the village on being confronted by the First Russian Grenadier Division, supported by artillery. The Russians took up a strong position about a knoll on which some guns were posted, and Poniatovski, not knowing that Konovnitzin had been driven from the Semyonovskaya heights, did not advance farther, fearing to be cut off from the French army. It was not until half-past ten, when Junot had appeared and engaged the Russians on his left, that Poniatovski drove Tuchkov back and took possession of the knoll.

In the meantime Prince Eugene had attacked the battery in the Russian centre, which was defended by **The Battle in the Centre** Raevski, the whole of whose second line had been sent to reinforce the defenders of the Semyonovskaya heights by order of Bagration. Raevski's troops, some dozen battalions in all, were disposed along the ravine in rear of the battery, so that from the right a flanking fire could be brought to bear on the attack. From the opening of the battle a sharp action had proceeded between the Russian skirmishers across the Semyonovka stream ahead of the battery, and Morand's troops. Broussier's division, crossing the Kalocha, also took part in the action ; and the French batteries soon forced the Russian skirmishers to retire from the stream to the hill. Broussier and Morand followed up the attack, Gerard's division remaining in reserve ; while Montbrun was ordered to cross and support Morand's attack. At about ten o'clock Broussier made an unsuccessful attempt to assault the battery, but was driven back.

The French now prepared a fresh attack by opening a heavy artillery fire, and at eleven o'clock the assault was renewed by Morand's troops, whose leading brigade under Bonamy drove the Russians out and captured their guns and earthwork, thus gaining a most important point in the centre of the enemy's position.

At this moment the Russian General Yermolov, Chief-of-the-Staff of the First Army, was passing along the rear of the captured battery with two batteries of horse artillery which he was leading to reinforce the left of the Semyonovskaya position. He saw what had happened, and at once turned his guns on the captured battery, and taking the first fresh battalion he could find, led it against the French, taking with him also the Russian troops that were streaming back from the captured position. Morand had not had time to confirm the success gained by his leading brigade when this attack took place. At the same time General Kreytz with three regiments of dragoons, supported by artillery fire, charged the remainder of Morand's troops. The French were driven out of the battery, forced back, and pursued for some distance; Montbrun was killed, and the divisional generals, Morand, Pajol and Defrance, were wounded, and Bonamy wounded and taken prisoner, the

French losing altogether in this attack on the Raevski battery some 3000 men.

It was now midday. On the left of the position the Russians had formed a new front. At nine o'clock General Baggevoot had received orders to proceed to that flank, and had started with his two divisions, leaving only his rifle regiments on the right flank in the grove and the bed of the Kalocha. On the way the corps was divided, one division being taken by Baggevoot to the left while the other under Prince Eugene of Wurtemberg was first directed against the captured Raevski battery, but on the battery being taken as above described, the Prince moved on to form a new line between that and Semyonovskaya, where he was joined by Barclay de Tolly. Here they formed squares to repulse the French cavalry, whose attacks have already been described, and having suffered heavily from the subsequent cannonade, the Prince moved his division to the left to the old Smolensk road.

Reinforcement of the Russian Left

Meanwhile Baggevoot had reached the left, and was supporting Shakhovski against Junot's Westphalians with four regiments, while the remainder of the division joined Tuchkov in an attack on Poniatovski. This was successful and the Poles were driven back on Utitza after a fierce struggle in which the gallant Tuchkov was mortally wounded.

Thus, at midday, after six hours' fighting, the Russians were still in possession of their original line with the exception of the part of it about Semyonovskaya. Some time previously an offensive movement had been undertaken from the Russian right against the troops left behind the Kalocha by the Viceroy Eugene.

At about midday the whole of Uvarov's 1st Cavalry Corps, 2500 strong, having crossed the Kalocha, together **Uvarov's Cavalry Charge** with Platov's Cossacks, drove back Ornano's cavalry, and appeared on Delzons' left flank near Borodino, but failed to accomplish anything further, although the movement had considerable effect on the course of the battle.

At one o'clock the Viceroy's troops received orders to renew the attack on Raevski's battery, while the Young Guard and the reserve cavalry moved to support him. The fire of seventy-six guns was brought to bear on the battery, and the attack was about to begin when Uvarov's cavalry created the diversion referred to above. This caused the return of a considerable portion of Eugene's corps across the river with a view to repel what was thought to be a serious attack on the French left and rear. But although Uvarov did not accomplish much, his movement had the effect of delaying for an hour the decisive attack on the Russian centre, while for a time it paralysed all movements on the French side and gave the Russians breathing-space in which to establish themselves in their new positions.

It was two o'clock. Arrangements were now made to renew the attack on Raevski's battery, while the French right was to press forward beyond Semyonovskaya. The Russians, seeing that the hostile forces were gathering for the attack, exchanged the shattered corps of Raevski for Osterman's corps, which moved into the first line with its right on the main road and its left towards Semyonovskaya. It appeared to their enemies as though they were about to make an offensive movement, and a mass of artillery was brought to bear upon them. But the Russian troops remained firm under this devastating cannonade, while their guns replied, and a general duel of artillery raged along the entire front, where on either side 800 guns vomited forth death upon their opponents.

Renewed attack on the Centre

The attack on the Raevski battery was led by Caulaincourt with some cavalry, followed by the divisions of Morand, Gerard and Broussier. On the Russian side Osterman was sustained by the 2nd and 3rd Cavalry Corps.

Caulaincourt charged the battery with strength and courage, overthrew some of the Russian infantry, and forced an entrance at the head of his cuirassiers, but was himself killed, while his horsemen suffered severely and would

Capture of Raevski's Battery

have been entirely destroyed. But the Viceroy Eugene's columns were swarming in; the redoubt was captured; its defenders being slain, and the Russian line was driven back behind the ravine in rear, after a final charge by Grouchy, who was forced to retire by the cavalry of the Russian guard.

It was now three o'clock. The French were at length in possession of the field of battle, but the Russians, driven back from their first position at all points, still showed a front behind the Semyonovka to the high-road about Gorki. Only the troops on both sides were exhausted, and the battle now became merely a cannonade.

Poniatovski, when he saw that Ney and Davout were successful, had in the meantime attacked the mamelon behind Utitza; and the Russians at that point, now under command of Baggevoot, fell back into line with the broken remnants of Bagration's troops at the source of the Semyonovka. The cannonade continued until nightfall, but the battle was practically at an end. **The Battle ends** Napoleon had still in hand the 19,000 men of his Guard, but did not employ them. He himself rode forward to Semyonovskaya at four o'clock, and returned to his camp at seven, when, "contrary to his usual demeanour, his face was heated, his hair in disorder, and his whole air one of fatigue."

At six o'clock in the evening the Russians occupied

positions as follows :—the 6th Infantry Corps was on the right flank at the battery near Gorki, from whence the first line extended in the direction of Semyonovskaya; the 4th Infantry Corps was on the left flank of the 6th; the remains of the Second Army were farther to the left; the 3rd and the greater part of the 2nd Infantry Corps under Baggevoot stood apart, on both sides of the old Smolensk road, in prolongation of the line occupied by the troops of the Second Army. The Cavalry Corps were in the second line, and the 5th Corps was in reserve. The position had no advantages for defence; behind it, at a distance of about two thousand yards, the route of retreat to Moscow lay parallel to it. An attack by the Guard must have had a decisive effect. The sun was still high when Murat sent General Belliard to Napoleon to ask for the co-operation of the Guard. Napoleon rode to the Semyonovskaya heights and thence to Raevski's battery. Everywhere he saw the Russians standing in expectation of a renewal of the battle. But the Emperor said : " I will not have my Guard destroyed. At a distance of eight hundred leagues from France one does not destroy one's last reserve."

<small>**Russian Position**</small>

The Russian loss amounted to some 44,000 men ; the French had not less than 28,000 casualties.

Knowing the disposition of both armies, it is not difficult to criticise the actions of the combatants at the battle of Borodino. The faulty occupation of the position by the Russians, who were weak on their left, where strength was essential, has already been noted. This was to some **Comments** extent remedied during the battle by the constant movement of troops from the right wing to the decisive points of the field. The position of the Russian Commander-in-Chief appears also to have been faulty. Kutuzov was inactive from age and decrepitude, and at Gorki he was little able to see what was going on or to exercise influence on the course of events. He was fortunate in having able and devoted subordinates and good staff officers. Uvarov's movement against the French left and rear would have been more effective had a force of all arms been employed, but no doubt every gun and every available man was required elsewhere. As it was, it exercised a considerable effect on the operations, delaying the final attack on the centre, and perhaps influencing Napoleon in his decision to retain the Guard in reserve.

Napoleon's plan of attack would probably have met with success had the assault on the Russian left been made in greater strength to begin with. But the battle was almost a purely frontal battle; for Poniatovski's movement against the left was in the first instance little more than a demonstration.

In some battles success depends upon the first shock; or it may depend upon effort concentrated at the end of the action. At Waterloo, for instance, the decisive moment for Wellington was when Blucher and his Prussians approached. At Borodino Napoleon was in vastly superior force on his right when the battle opened; that was the decisive moment when the concentration of strength against the Russian left would have decided the battle; but the somewhat desultory nature of the attack and its distribution gave time for the weak Russian left to hold out until they were reinforced by 40,000 men who had been erroneously posted on their right.

The troops of Ney and Davout might well have been employed in their full strength in the first attack on the Russian left, while Eugene "held" the centre. When Eugene did attack, his attack should have been carried out, not with Morand's division only, as it was at ten o'clock, but with his entire strength, as it was between two and three o'clock. Eventually, but too late, the whole Russian line was forced from the centre at Raevski's redoubt, from Semyonovskaya and from beyond Utitza. This was done against the entire strength of the Russian army. How much more easily, then, it might have been accomplished by a decisive attack before the enemy had been able to correct the faulty disposition of his troops.

The columns of attack were disposed in great depth. A wider distribution would have facilitated the turning of the Russian left.

Napoleon has been blamed for not employing the 19,000 men of his Guard to confirm the victory. Certainly he would seem to have acted in this against his own maxim—" Generals who save troops for the next day are always beaten," as he did in the general conduct of the battle contrary to his other maxim: "Never make a frontal attack upon a position which you can circumvent." But the circumstances have to be considered. There were still in view behind the enemy's left 10,000 men in reserve. That these consisted of the Moscow militia armed with pikes was not known to the French Emperor. The strategical situation has to be taken into account. At a distance of 800 leagues from France; in a hostile country, short of transport and supplies, the position of the French army in case of reverse would have been one of supreme danger. But it may be doubted whether the old Napoleon, the General of Italy, of Marengo, of Austerlitz, and of Jena would have been so cautious. He would surely have used his reserves up to the last man to secure a decisive victory.

When all has been considered it certainly appears that Napoleon did not in this battle display the greatness of conception and vigour in execution that marked his previous victories. He showed unwonted caution. He did not dominate the issue as was his former habit. This has by some been ascribed to the state of his health. But, although suffering from indisposition, he preserved all his faculties. The problem was a simple one—to destroy the Russian left, and every effort should have been directed to the attainment of that object at the beginning of the day.

At the same time we must remember what Napoleon himself said in Italy in 1797: " Health is indispensable in war "; and, a few years later : " There is but one season for war ; I shall be fit for it six years longer, and then I shall myself be obliged to stop." He had passed the limit set by himself when the highest efficiency could be expected.

CHAPTER XI

THE OCCUPATION OF MOSCOW

Russian Retreat—The Russians abandon Moscow—Napoleon enters Moscow—The Burning of the City—Russian March to Podolsk—Pursuit by French Advanced Guard—French Movements—Napoleon proposes Peace—Measures for the Future—Napoleon's Appreciation of the Situation—The Question of Retreat—Action at Vinkovo—Evacuation of Moscow—Operations on the Dwina—Events in Volhynia

AFTER the battle of Borodino, Kutuzov decided to retreat. His army, reduced to some 50,000 men, was in no condition **Russian Retreat** to make a further stand. On the morning of the 8th September the Russians retreated before dawn, and halted beyond Mozhaisk, leaving a rearguard under Platov, which remained on the field of battle until eleven o'clock.

They were pursued by an advanced guard under Murat, consisting of the cavalry and Dufour's (late Friand's) division. Mortier with the Young Guard and Davout's corps followed, and after them Ney and the Old Guard. Poniatovski marched by the old Smolensk road, and afterwards turned to the right towards Borisov, and the Viceroy Eugene moved on Ruza to the left of the main army. Junot remained on the field of battle to look after the wounded, afterwards halting at

Mozhaisk until Napoleon's army returned thither from Moscow.

On the 8th Napoleon remained in his camp at Shivardino; "he seemed overwhelmed by fatigue; from time to time he clasped his hands violently over his crossed knees, and was frequently heard to repeat with a kind of convulsive movement—'Moscow! Moscow!'"

That day the Russian army retreated to Zemlino, while the rearguard remained at Mozhaisk until driven out next day by Murat. They left behind 10,000 wounded, who were turned into the streets by the French to make room for their own sick and wounded. On the 10th September the Russians retreated to Krutitzi, and their rearguard, now commanded by Miloradovich, made a stand at Krimskoye. The rearguard held their own when Murat attacked them, and did not retire until they had suffered a loss of 2000 men. The French casualties were no less in number. This day Kutuzov enrolled 14,000 men of the Moscow militia to form third ranks in his regiments. On the 11th he reached Bolshaya Viazyoma and next day Mamonova. He had been engaged in reorganising his army during the retreat from Borodino. Those infantry regiments which had less than 300 men under arms were formed into battalions; the 2nd and 3rd Cavalry Corps were formed into one corps under Baron Korf. Konovnitzin was appointed to command the 3rd Infantry Corps in place of Tuchkov, killed in the battle.

On the 13th September the Russian army bivouacked outside Moscow, two versts from the Dragomilov gate. In view of the slow pursuit Kutuzov feared that the Viceroy Eugene might turn his right and occupy Moscow in his rear. Winzingerode's detachment, reinforced by a regiment of hussars and two of Cossacks, was directed to guard against such a movement. Winzingerode had been operating in rear of the French, and was at Ruza, north of Mozhaisk, on the 8th September. Finding himself close to the Viceroy Eugene's encampment, he made a night march, got ahead of him on the Moscow road, and was then posted on the Vladimir road.

Kutuzov in the first instance intended to give battle again under the walls of Moscow. A position was taken up and partly entrenched, the right in front of the village of Fili, the left on the Vorobyovia Gori—the Sparrow Hills. But it was represented to the Russian Commander-in-Chief that in a position so unfavourable defeat was certain. He decided to abandon Moscow and continue his retreat; but as he did not desire to take the entire responsibility of abandoning the ancient capital, he called a council of war. The council, however, were mostly in favour of fighting, though Barclay de Tolly indicated the futility of courting certain defeat, when Moscow must be lost in any case, and the Russian army would in addition be rendered useless for further operations. Kutuzov gave orders for the retreat. The army was to retire by the Riazan road and then cross over to the Kaluga road. Supplies had been collected at Serpukhov, from whence they could be distributed with equal facility on either road. Count Rastopchin, the Governor of Moscow, reported that most of the inhabitants had already left the city. Those who remained were ordered by Kutuzov to be sent to Riazan. Rastopchin reported to the Emperor that all the commisariat and arsenal had been removed. But this was not the fact, for over 100 guns, 18,000 small arms, powder, and other supplies were left to the enemy.

Moscow is the heart of Russia. Upon its time-worn walls broods the spirit of a thousand years of veneration. **The Russians abandon Moscow** Within rise a thousand spires of varied colour and Oriental aspect. In its hundreds of sacred edifices are sheltered the icons—the sacred images—before which a primitive people bent in reverential homage. But the Russians decided to abandon their ancient capital. The remainder of the population left on the 13th and 14th September, and before dawn on the latter date the Russian army began the march through the city. Their baggage had been despatched during the night. The troops followed by way of the Dragomilov gate, preceded by the cavalry, the whole army marching in one long column to the exit by the Kolomen gate. They continued their march to the village of Panki, seventeen versts distant. The rearguard under Miloradovich followed, and would have had to fight with Murat's advanced guard in the town had not an agreement been arrived at between the opposing commanders to admit of peaceful evacuation.

Meanwhile the French army was drawing near Moscow; on the night of the 13th the main body was at Perkushkovo. The flanking columns were almost abreast—Poniatovski at Likova on the new Kaluga road, and the Viceroy Eugene at Buzaeva, marching by the Zvenigorod road on the right bank of the Moscow river. The French advanced guard entered practically in touch with the rearguard of the retreating army.

Napoleon passed the night of the 13th September at Viazyoma, forty versts from Moscow. At dawn he set out in a carriage, but later mounted his horse as the road at one point was impracticable owing to the destruction of a bridge. At two o'clock in the afternoon the Emperor ascended the Poklonnaya Gora (Mount of Salutation) and obtained his first view of Moscow. He dismounted, and examined the city for some time with the aid of a telescope, while his secretary and Russian interpreter, Lelorgne, who knew the place well, pointed out the principal features. He appeared pleased, and exclaimed: "So that is at last the famous city!" adding, "It was time!" A cannon shot was the signal for the army to move on. Napoleon rode to the Dragomilov gate. With shouts of "Long live the

Emperor! Long live Napoleon!" the French soldiers entered the Russian capital. Napoleon awaited in vain the expected deputation at the Dragomilov gate. "What," he exclaimed, "Moscow empty! What an unheard of thing; go and bring me the *boyars*!" But there remained only some gaol-birds, let loose from the prisons, and a few foreigners. No one else received the conqueror. The mighty actor on the world's stage appeared before an empty house! Not thus had he been received at Milan, Vienna, Berlin and Madrid! Already ominous columns of smoke were to be seen rising from the houses. The incendiaries were at work. Napoleon took up his residence in the Kremlin. He was driven forth by flames, and moved to the Petrovski Palace. In a few days the greater part of Moscow was reduced to ashes. At first the Russians accused the invaders of this act of vandalism. Afterwards it was claimed as a patriotic deed on the part of the Governor, Count Rastopchin, and the inhabitants. It was more probably the work of marauders. Moscow, mainly built of wood, was lighted easily and burnt quickly. If the burning of Moscow was a premeditated act, it is not easy to see what was to be gained by it. If it was designed to show the invaders that their enemy was implacable and would never come to terms, it might, had they so taken it, have warned them in time to effect a safe retreat. Or it might have caused them to

The Burning of the City

advance at once on Kaluga. To burn Moscow in the middle of September could serve but little purpose. There were supplies more ample than could be destroyed. To have arranged for incendiary fires at the end of October would have been to deprive the French of quarters on the approach of winter, or forced them to retreat when the climatic conditions were most severe.

It is a curious circumstance that a Belgian named Smidt proposed to assist in the destruction of the invading army with a balloon or flying machine, from which bombs and rockets were to be discharged. His project was seriously considered by the Government, but came to nothing. He and his balloon were removed to Nijni Novgorod when the Grand Army approached Moscow.

It is a question whether the French were wise in not harassing the Russians during their evacuation of the city. For Napoleon to refuse battle must have increased the steadfastness of the Russian Government, as it pointed to the exhaustion of their enemies. No doubt he did not wish to lose more men, while he counted on peace following on the occupation of the capital.

On the day of the French occupation of Moscow the Russian army marched fifteen versts on the Riazan road to the village of Panki; the rearguard under Miloradovich halted less than half that distance at Viazovka. A halt was made to cover the escape of the inhabitants of Moscow. The

Russian March to Podolsk

march was resumed on the 16th September, and next day after the passage of the Moskva River at Borovski Most, where the rearguard, now composed of fresh troops under Raevski, was left, Kutuzov executed a flank movement by forced marches and reached Podolsk on the 19th. During this movement the right flank was covered by the Pakhra River. The rearguard, having destroyed the bridge at Borovski, marched by night, leaving Ephrimov with two Cossack regiments on the Riazan road.

On the 21st the army reached Krasnaya Pakhra, where it was covered by a detachment under Miloradovich, posted at Desna. It was at this time that the Russians began those partisan operations with detachments of Cossacks that contributed to the destruction of the invading army, by acting on their line of communications, attacking convoys, and finally by harassing the retreating columns.

The French vanguard under Sebastiani had meanwhile been sent on by Murat, who remained in Moscow, and had followed the Russians down the Riazan road. Sebastiani mistook Ephrimov's Cossacks for the Russian rearguard, and marched as far as Bronnitzi, whilst Murat, completely deceived, informed Napoleon that the Russian army had dispersed, leaving only Cossacks. But on reaching Bronnitzi, Sebastiani became convinced that he had been led astray.

Pursuit by French Advanced Guard

Napoleon heard on the night of the 21st September that his advanced guard had lost sight of the Russian army, and that Cossacks had appeared on the Mozhaisk road and attacked his transport. He at once sent Poniatovski's corps to Podolsk, and directed Murat to take command of these troops and those on the Riazan road and follow the Russians. Bessieres was sent with a corps of observation on the road to Tula, whence he subsequently moved on to the old Kaluga road. Some cavalry, subsequently reinforced by guns and Broussier's division, was sent towards Mozhaisk, and Napoleon himself prepared to move in order to drive the Russians beyond the Oka.

The Russian flank movement from the Riazan to the Kaluga road enabled them to cover Kaluga, where there were great stores of provisions, and Tula with its arms factory, and at the same time to maintain communication with the southern regions of the Empire, whence all necessary supplies could be drawn. It also placed them in a position to act against the enemy's communications, and detachments of cavalry were appointed for this purpose.

The French army, meanwhile, remained for some time in inaction in Moscow, where Napoleon had up to the 26th

French Movements September no reliable information as to the position of the Russians. Poniatovski was ordered to Podolsk on the 24th September, and next day

Murat moved to that place with all his cavalry. At the same time Bessieres approached Desna. These movements forced back the Russian detachments, which drew the French cavalry away from the main Russian army.

There are three roads leading from Moscow to Kaluga, the shortest of which passes through Krasnaya-Pakhra and Tarutino. Kutuzov decided to take up and strengthen a position at the latter place, there awaiting reinforcements and the development of events before undertaking any further operations with the main army.

Napoleon had hoped that the occupation of the capital would lead the enemy to sue for peace. He lingered in Moscow in this expectation, sent Lauriston, formerly ambassador in St Petersburg, to negotiate an armistice with Kutuzov and make overtures to the Tzar. Kutuzov temporised; despatched an envoy to the Tzar with the French proposals, which were, however, indefinite, and at the same time urged Alexander to make no terms. Napoleon had mistaken the Tzar's character. That monarch displayed unexpected firmness and decision, and adhered to his previous resolution, that he would not consider terms of peace so long as a French soldier remained on Russian soil, nor would he communicate with the French Emperor.

Napoleon proposes Peace

The long halt in Moscow after the hardships and

privations through which the soliders had passed, the evacuation of the city by its inhabitants, and the fires by which the place was devastated reacted on the discipline of the troops. The men abandoned themselves to disorder, and marauding did not cease until the Emperor took stringent measures to restore discipline when he returned from the Petrovski Palace to the Kremlin. This was on the 19th September after the conflagration ceased.

In the meantime Napoleon was obliged to consider his measures for the future. He had several alternatives.

Measures for the Future
The possibility of remaining in the Moscow for the winter had to be immediately dismissed. He might move northwards at once, and threaten St Petersburg, in the hope of thus forcing the Russians to conclude peace. Or he could march north-west to the Lower Dwina, where he would be in a position to menace St Petersburg, and at the same time avoid the appearance of a retreat, which would demoralise his army and have a dangerous effect in Prussia and throughout Europe generally. Or he could retreat by Kaluga towards Warsaw and Grodno through a region that had not yet been ravaged by war. Situated as he was, with a hostile army of constantly increasing strength in the neighbourhood, it would have been foolhardy to march direct on St Petersburg, and risk being cut off from his base. But a movement towards the Lower

Dwina, supported by Victor, who could march with 40,000 men from Polotzk to Velikiya Luki, whilst the Emperor advanced on Velizh, would open the way for further operations. He could then have moved on Novgorod with 140,000 men, or at the worst could have retreated towards Polotzk and Vitebsk, where he would have been supported by Oudinot and Macdonald on the Lower Dwina. As for the southern project, Kutuzov already barred the way to Kaluga. The French army was scarcely in a condition to fight another battle with an enemy whose strength was being continuously augmented.

The Emperor's appreciation of the situation is recorded in the following undated notes, probably dictated by him during the first days of October :—

Napoleon's Appreciation of the Situation
"(1) Since the enemy is moving to the Kiev road, their intention is evident; they expect reinforcements from the Moldavian army. To march against them would mean to manœuvre in the direction of the reinforcements and winter in cantonments without any *point d'appui*, with our flanks exposed, while the enemy's flanks and rear would be secure. Moscow, abandoned by its inhabitants and burnt, is no longer of any use to us; the city can no longer harbour our sick and wounded; if the supplies there are once exhausted, it can furnish no fresh ones, nor assist us in establishing order in the country.

"(2) A movement on Kaluga would only be excusable with a view of retreating from that place to Smolensk.

"(3) If the army is to retreat to Smolensk, would there be any reason in seeking the enemy and exposing ourselves to the loss of some thousands of men on a march which would appear like a retreat, and in the face of an army well acquainted with the country and having many secret agents and numerous light cavalry? Even though the French army were victorious, such a movement would place it at a disadvantage, since a rearguard loses men daily, whilst a vanguard gains strength. Moreover a rearguard has to abandon a battlefield daily, and loses its wounded, stragglers and camp followers.

"(4) To these considerations must be added the probability of the enemy fortifying themselves in a strong position, and, the heads of the reinforcing columns having arrived, causing us a loss of 3000 or 4000 wounded; this would look like defeat. A retrograde movement for a hundred leagues, burthened with wounded, and harassed by encounters represented by the enemy as victories, would ensure him, even though beaten, the advantage of public opinion.

"(5) If we desire to retreat in order to occupy winter quarters in Poland, would it be advisable to retreat by the direct route by which we advanced? We should not be harassed by the enemy; we are well acquainted with the road, which is shorter by five days' march; we can march as rapidly as we like and meet our supplies half-way from Smolensk. However, the army could easily carry a fortnight's flour, and we could reach Smolensk without being obliged to forage. We could even stop at Vyazma as long as we wished, and procure supplies by extending right and left.

"We are conquerors, our organisation is perfect, and if we had to fight and carry our wounded, we should be in the same position as during the advance, when the advanced guard had some wounded. It is true difficulties may arise with regard to fodder, but we could procure that within two or three leagues, and the difficulty would not be serious.

"(1) There can be no doubt but that, if Smolensk and Vitebsk were districts like Koenigsberg and Elbing, the first would be the most sensible plan, namely, to march to a favourable country, go into winter quarters, and recruit the army.

"(2) In such case, however, we cannot conceal from ourselves that the war would be greatly protracted, but it would still be more protracted if we chose inhospitable districts such as Smolensk and Vitebsk, which offer scanty resources and are little suited for eight months in winter quarters.

"What ought to be done :

"(I.) What results are to be attained ? (i) To quarter

the Emperor as near France as possible, and satisfy the country that he would be in the midst of a friendly population in winter quarters. (ii) To admit of the army being cantoned in a friendly country, near its supplies of clothing and equipment.

"(iii) To occupy a position threatening St Petersburg, and so support the Emperor in his negotiations for peace. (iv) To maintain our military reputation at the height to which it has been raised by this victorious campaign.

"(II.) A manœuvre combining these four conditions would undoubtedly be perfect.

"This manœuvre would be as follows :—

"The Duke of Belluno (Victor) with his corps reinforced by four battalions of Saxons, two battalions of Westphalians, two or three battalions of Illyrians, and two battalions of the 129th Infantry Regiment, bringing it up to a force of nearly 40,000 men, would leave Smolensk the first day of the operation, and march to Velizh and Velikya Luki, where it would arrive on the eighth or ninth day ; from Velikya Luki the Duke of Belluno would take his line of operations on Polotzk and Vitebsk. Marshal St Cyr, leaving his position at Polotzk, would reinforce him in six days.

"The Duke of Tarentum (Macdonald) would send him, from the environs of Dinaburg, a brigade of infantry.

"The Duke of Belluno, as the senior, would command all these troops united at Velikya Luki, where, on the tenth day from the commencement of the movement, an army of 70,000 men would be concentrated. At Velikya Luki the army would draw supplies from Polotzk and Vitebsk.

"On the day when the Duke of Belluno began his movement, the Emperor would leave Moscow with the army and march on Velizh by Voskresensk, so that the head of the army would reach Velizh on the tenth day, and its rear on the thirteenth or fourteenth day. At Velizh the army would draw supplies equally from Vitebsk and Polotzk. Thus, while the Duke of Belluno menaced St Petersburg from his position at Velikya Luki, the army would be behind him on the Dwina; the 3rd Corps and the corps of the Duke of Abrantes (Junot), numbering at least 15,000 men, would march from Moscow and Mozhaisk on Smolensk by way of Vyazma.

"All the cavalry and infantry regiments on the march to join the army would be directed on Vitebsk and Velizh, to meet the army and incorporate themselves with it on arrival. The Emperor, with the Cavalry of the Guard, the Old Guard and the Young Guard, would be at the head of the army, in order to be in a position to support the Duke of Belluno in case of necessity. Finally, on the twelfth day of the operation, that is to say, of the movement of the army, the position would be as follows :—

"The Duke of Belluno with Marshal St Cyr and one of the Duke of Tarentum's brigades, forming a corps of

60,000 or 70,000 men, would be at Velikya Luki, having an advanced guard several marches on the road to St Petersburg.

"The Emperor with the Guard and the Viceroy's corps, 40,000 men, would be at Velizh.

"The King of Naples, with his troops and the corps of the Prince of Eckmuhl (Davout), would form a kind of rearguard or corps of observation three days in rear, in the direction of Byeloi.

"The hostile army could not enter Moscow until the sixth day of the operation, and General Wittgenstein would already be in retreat; the Duke of Belluno would have passed the Dwina, and would be menacing St Petersburg. The hostile army, arrived at Moscow six days after our departure, would follow our movement to deliver battle at Velizh, and then the King of Naples, the Prince of Eckmuhl (Davout) and the Duke of Elchingen (Ney) would have joined us, while the reinforcements expected from Moldavia by the enemy would not have joined him and would have lost themselves on the main roads. He would then arrive before us with very inferior forces which would diminish daily, whilst ours would be augmented.

"The Duke of Belluno, five days after his arrival at Velikya Luki, reinforced by the corps marching with the Emperor, could in case of necessity advance to Novgorod. St Petersburg being thus threatened, one must believe that the enemy would make peace, and if the circumstances of the movements of the enemy did not tend to advance, we could remain at Velikya Luki."

As these projects did not fructify it is unnecessary to comment on them, but it may be remarked that the whole scheme bears an appearance of unreality, of a desire to mould circumstances in accordance with Napoleon's wishes, and that it makes several unwarrantable assumptions.

Napoleon still remained in Moscow, awaiting a reply to his proposals from St Petersburg. Twenty days had elapsed since his entry into the ancient capital of Russia. It was imperative to consider the question of retreat. He has been blamed for hesitating so long, for winter was approaching. But in criticising the Emperor, factors of the widest range have to be taken into consideration. It was not to be supposed that Napoleon would be willing to retreat except as a last resort. Much as his army had suffered in strength and discipline during the advance, he knew it would suffer still more in a retreat. He had scarcely sufficient horses to mount half his cavalry, and to draw those guns the greater number of which may to-day be seen in the Kremlin, where they were taken when abandoned on the march. Europe might rise in his rear, and he had unfriendly elements in his army—Austrians, Prussians

The Question of Retreat

and Westphalians—who would be ready to abandon a lost cause. Events in Spain caused him anxiety, for Wellington had entered Madrid after the battle of Salamanca.

In addition he feared for his line of communications. The main Russian army was in a position to threaten it. The army of Moldavia under Chichagov had advanced against Schwarzenberg, and forced that general to retire behind the Bug. Warsaw and Vilna were threatened. Steinheil's corps from Finland had reinforced the enemy in Livonia, where they were now superior to Macdonald. To meet the situation, Victor had reached Smolensk, followed by Baraguey d'Hilliers with 10,000 men. Austria was requested to reinforce Schwarzenberg, and Prussia asked to send a division to Macdonald.

But it was out of the question to remain much longer in Moscow. To winter there, a course which had been considered, was impossible. Apart from the distance from France, the communications were insecure, although hitherto partisan operations had had little effect on them. But even if sufficient provisions could be obtained in Moscow for the men, forage would not be available for cavalry and artillery horses and cattle during the long and severe winter.

Meanwhile Murat was with the advanced guard about Vinkovo on the River Chernishna, sixty versts from Moscow. His isolated position led Kutuzov to attack him. Murat had not more than 20,000 men, including 8000 cavalry, with 187 guns. His troops were reduced by hardship and privation, and he occupied a position unfavourable for defence. The negotiations he had engaged in with Kutuzov led him to hope for early peace. It is said that he had been lulled into security by an understanding, amounting to an armistice, which had been concluded with the Russian commander. The existence of this armistice is denied by Russian authorities, who aver that it referred only to outposts. At any rate Kutuzov was quite capable of undertaking hostilities in any circumstances, should a good chance of success present itself, notwithstanding his inherent unwillingness to enter on active operations. A disposition to remain always on the defensive appears to be a constant characteristic of the Russian race.

Action at Vinkovo

Kutuzov was at length induced to attack Murat's army. Reconnaissances had revealed that the French, either through laxness or trusting to the armistice, were not keeping up their protective services efficiently. A forest on the left of the French encampment was not watched or patrolled. On the 18th October the Russians advanced, the main army to make a frontal attack, while a strong corps under Bennigsen traversed the forest on the French left by a night march with a view to attacking that flank. The manœuvre was badly executed, though well conceived, the flank attack arriving too late, and although the French lost a general, some 1500 men and 38 guns, the action was in no way decisive. On the Russian side Baggevoot was killed, and there were 1000 casualties.

Napoleon had already made arrangements to retreat. He concentrated his forces, and on the 15th October his light cavalry and Broussier's division, which were at Beryozki on the road to Mozhaisk, crossed over to Fominskoye on the new Kaluga road, whilst the Viceroy Eugene's cavalry of the Guard moved to Sharpova on the Mozhaisk road. Napoleon inspected his troops daily, and on the 18th was engaged in reviewing Ney's corps in the Kremlin, when he heard the ominous sound of a heavy cannonade in the direction of Murat's advanced guard. Soon an aide-de-camp arrived from Murat with news that the Russians had assumed the offensive. He at once stopped the review and gave immediate orders for the march.

Evacuation of Moscow

The Emperor's plan was to turn the left flank of the Russian army by marching first along the old Kaluga road which leads through Tarutino, and effecting a junction with Murat. Then, crossing over to the new Kaluga road to march through Borovsk and by way of Kaluga to Smolensk. His immediate object was to get to Maloyaroslavetz before Kutuzov became aware of his project. It was necessary to conceal the movement as long as possible, and it was perhaps for this purpose that

Colonel Berthemy was sent to renew negotiations with Kutuzov, with a letter from Berthier in which it was proposed " to take measures to give the war a character in accordance with accepted measures, and to stop the laying waste of the country, which was as harmful to Russia as it was distasteful to the Emperor Napoleon." Kutuzov, as usual temporising, wrote that there had not yet been time to receive a reply to the despatch sent to the Tzar by Prince Volkonski.

While the events that have been narrated were taking place, there was considerable activity in the theatre of war where the wings of the Grand Army were engaged, both on the Dwina and in Volhynia.

Operations on the Dwina

After the first battle of Polotzk, Wittgenstein's troops were disposed from the 23rd August to the 16th October with headquarters at Sivoshin on the right bank of the Drissa stream, and the reserve and cavalry corps at Sokolishchi. With the object of holding the French on the Drissa, Wittgenstein strengthened the defences of Sebezh, where his depots were stationed; and detachments were posted at Kamenetz, to observe Macdonald, and on the Svolna and the road from Polotzk to Nevel to cover the front of the corps. He thus protected St Petersburg by covering the roads leading from the Dwina to Novgorod and Pskov.

Marshal St Cyr did not venture to attack Wittgenstein,

having an exaggerated idea of his strength, while his energies were largely directed to obtaining supplies, for want of which, however, his troops suffered considerably. In September Wittgenstein received considerable reinforcements, mostly militia, amounting in all to 15,000 men. During the period under review the only hostilities on the Dwina consisted of partisan operations. Later in October Wittgenstein received orders to attack the French at Polotzk, and drive them towards Sventziani; he was then to leave the pursuit to Steinheil's corps, and to co-operate with Chichagov in cutting off the retreat of Napoleon's army. The result of these operations will be seen in the chapter dealing with the passage of the Berezina.

On conclusion of the treaty with Sweden, Steinheil's corps of 10,000 men, which had been posted in Finland, was ordered to Riga, where it arrived on the 22nd September.

Macdonald had remained inactive at Dinaburg with the 12,000 men of Grandjean's division, while the Prussian troops under York were in observation before Riga, the garrison of which, under General Essen, made several sorties in July and August.

Marshal Victor, with the corps constituting the reserve of the Grand Army, reached Tilsit on the 9th August. He had 30,000 men. This corps set out from Tilsit at the end of August, and, marching by way of Kovno and

Vilna, arrived at Smolensk on the 28th September, after suffering considerable loss both in men and horses from want of provisions, and from disease. At Smolensk matters were not much better, as supplies were of inferior quality.

The arrival of reinforcements for Wittgenstein obliged Victor to take measures to support St Cyr. With this object Daendels' division left Smolensk for Babinovichy on the 11th October. At the same time Partouneaux's division was posted at Mstislavl, for convenience of supply, and Gerard's division remained in Smolensk. Victor now had about 25,000 men.

After the indecisive action at Gorodechno related in Chapter VI., Tormassov retreated behind the Styr on the 29th August. His main forces were posted at Lutzk, with advanced detachments under Count Lambert and Chaplitz, the first from the Austrian frontier to Lutzk, the second from Lutzk to Kolki.

Events in Volhynia

Schwarzenberg and Reynier stood between the Styr and the Turya, with advanced posts at Torchin and Charukov.

The Russians were in a safe position, the Styr being unfordable from the point where it crosses the Austrian frontier until its junction with the Pripet, while all the bridges had been destroyed; and their movements behind the river were concealed by the forest. On their side, in open and marshy country, Schwarzenberg and

Reynier contented themselves with holding the Russian army behind the Styr, and covering the communications of Napoleon's army on the side of Volhynia.

On the 19th September Admiral Chichagov, released from operations in Wallachia by the peace with Turkey, arrived on the Styr. His army numbered 35,000 men and 204 guns. This brought the strength of the Russians in Volhynia up to over 60,000 men, opposed to Schwarzenberg and Reynier's 43,000.

On the 22nd and 23rd September the combined Russian forces crossed the Styr at several points. The allied troops retired in front of them, crossed the Turya, and concentrated at Liuboml, where they took up a position behind a canal, after several skirmishes between the protective detachments. The Russians followed, crossed the canal on the 30th, Schwarzenberg retiring in front of them. Chichagov now assumed command of the troops in Volhynia, and Tormassov left for Kutuzov's headquarters.

Schwarzenberg retired on Brest-Litovsk, and on the 4th October took up a position between the Rukavetz and Lyesna streams in front of that place. The Russians followed, crossed the Mukhavetz between Brest and Bulkov, and at the same time occupied Kobrin with a part of their forces after driving out the enemy's detachment. Dispositions were made to attack Schwarzenberg on the 11th October, but the Austrian General retired behind the

Lyesna and retreated first to Volchin, and then, being pursued, crossed the Bug between Melnik and Drogichin on the 12th. Chichagov occupied Brest Litovsk. Thus the allied corps were driven into the Grand Duchy of Warsaw, and the road to the Berezina was laid open to the Russian advance.

Chichagov remained inactive at Brest for a fortnight, to collect supplies, but sent detachments into the Grand Duchy to seize the magazines and to harass the enemy.

Schwarzenberg, after the action at Gorodechno, might perhaps have followed up his success and tried to deal Tormassov another blow before his junction with Chichagov. But this would in all probability have been ineffective, for the Russian would merely have retired before him until the junction was completed. His retirement on Warsaw instead of towards Minsk, a direction that would have brought him into communication with Napoleon's army, is perhaps more open to criticism; he appears to have considered first the retention of the shortest line of communication with Austria, on which there were ample supplies, in place of co-operating with the main army of invasion. He thus did not fulfil his rôle, which was to protect, on the right flank, the communications of the army.

The curtain was now about to rise on the last act of this great drama, than which the history of the world can scarcely show a greater human tragedy.

CHAPTER XII

FROM MOSCOW TO MALOYAROSLAVETZ

March of the Grand Army—Kutuzov leaves Tarutino—Maloyaroslavetz—Advance or Retreat ?—Retreat—Comments

ON the evacuation of Moscow the French army numbered over 105,000 men and 569 guns. Of these there were nearly 90,000 infantry. The sick and wounded had been despatched as far as possible by the direct road to Mozhaisk, which was occupied by Junot. Mortier was left in Moscow; he had orders to remain in occupation until the 23rd, when he was to blow up the Kremlin and public buildings and march to Vereya, where he would be in a position to maintain communication between the main army and Junot.

March of the Grand Army

Napoleon left Moscow on the 19th October. Prince Eugene's corps formed the advanced guard, with Ney immediately behind; then followed the Old Guard, two divisions of Davout's corps, a division of the Young Guard accompanying headquarters, the treasure, and waggons laden with trophies; finally Morand's division of Davout's corps and Colbert's brigade of cavalry of the

Guard. The light cavalry marched on either flank of the column. These flanking troops and the rearguard had orders to burn the villages *en route*. Napoleon himself arrived at Troitzkoye at four o'clock in the afternoon ; and the advanced guard reached Viyatutinka at the same time.

The march of the French army from Moscow had the appearance of the migration of a people ; the impedimenta occupying a length of many miles. There were 2000 artillery carriages. Each company had an equipment of two or three carts for the transport of provisions. There was a confused assemblage of carriages, waggons and carts of every description, and even wheelbarrows, laden with booty. There were trophies of Russian, Turkish and Persian flags. There was a motley crowd of followers, including many women and children.

Such were the encumbrances with which this army set out on a march that was to be perhaps the most difficult and terrible that has ever been attempted.

On the 20th October Napoleon remained at Troitzkoye, while the advanced guard, having reached Krasnaya Pakhra, took a cross-country track to Fominskoye on the new Kaluga road. The same day Ney's corps effected a junction with Murat on the Mocha, while Poniatovski fell in in rear of the advanced guard under Eugene, and was afterwards directed on Vereya.

On the 21st Napoleon reached Pleskovo, near Ignatovo, and Eugene—Fominskoye. Thus the movement towards Borovsk continued. Orders were given to Junot to march on Vyazma. Mortier had left Moscow for Mozhaisk on the 23rd, after fulfilling his instructions, although fortunately not much damage was done to the Kremlin. He took with him General Winzingerode, who, foolishly venturing into Moscow with an aide-de-camp, was taken prisoner.

Napoleon galloped on to Borovsk on the 23rd, and ordered Eugene, who had arrived the previous evening, to continue the movement on Maloyaroslavetz. But Eugene observed the movement of Russian troops on his left, and moved slowly, thinking that the Emperor might be attacked at Borovsk, when he would be obliged to retrace his footsteps.

Kutuzov, hearing of the march of Eugene on Borovsk, but unaware that Napoleon was retreating, thought this an isolated movement, and conceived the idea of attacking these 10,000 men, detaching for this purpose 25,000 men under Dokhturov. But Dokhturov received information from Seslavin's Cossacks of the march of the whole French army, and changed his direction to Maloyaroslavetz. The Russian Commander-in-Chief, on this news, struck camp at Tarutino on the 24th October, and also marched on Maloyaroslavetz, which Dokhturov occupied on the 24th,

Kutuzov leaves Tarutino

after expelling Eugene's advanced guard. Kutuzov had 97,000 men and 622 guns.

The town of Maloyaroslavetz stands upon a height overlooking the River Luzha on the north, from which direction the French were approaching. Beyond the town is a lofty plain surrounded by forest, traversed by roads from Kaluga and Tarutino. Delzons, who commanded Prince Eugene's advanced guard, had occupied the town on the evening of the 23rd with two battalions only, fearing to push his whole force beyond the river and defile on the edge of a precipice down which he might be driven by a night attack. At daybreak Dokhturov attacked and drove the French out of the town and back on to the division below. Prince Eugene was some six miles distant when the sound of the guns warned him of the action. He hurried forward with his remaining forces to support Delzons, who was with difficulty maintaining his hold on the bank of the Luzha, in a position exposed to the fire of the Russians on the heights above. The Prince ordered an attack, and the French pressed over the bridge across the river, drove back the masses of Russians who filled the ravine which led up to the town, and soon their bayonets glittered on the heights above. But here Delzons was killed, and his troops, disheartened, hesitated and fell back.

Reinforcements were now coming up on both sides. The battle continued throughout the day, the town being taken and retaken again and again. But the Russians were more numerous and continued to arrive. They occupied a strong and commanding position, and it was only after the exhaustion of all his troops that Eugene finally held the town, while the enemy assembled their forces on the road to Kaluga, between Maloyaroslavetz and the forest. Towards evening the whole French army arrived near the scene of action, and two of Davout's divisions were moved forward to support Eugene.

The two armies were now facing each other, Kutuzov barring the road to Kaluga, by which Napoleon had **Advance or Retreat?** intended to retreat through Yelnya on Smolensk. His expressed intention had been "to fight a battle should the enemy think of covering Kaluga." The Emperor had his headquarters at Gorodnya, some miles in rear. Napoleon now showed an indecision and a want of resolution that were new to him. He summoned the marshals, and asked their opinion as to "whether it was to the advantage of the army to fight or to avoid battle." The generals advised a retreat either direct on Smolensk or through Mozhaisk. It was the morning of the 25th, and the Emperor rode forward to reconnoitre the enemy's position. Soon after he started, some thousands of Platov's Cossacks rode close up to Napoleon, who was only saved by the presence of mind of his staff and the timely arrival of the cavalry of the Guard, who extricated him when he and his suite were surrounded and had drawn their swords to defend themselves. The Emperor spent the day in reconnoitring the Russian position, and returned to Gorodnya without having come to a decision. He certainly had reason to hesitate. Kutuzov had 90,000 men and 600 guns drawn up to bar his passage. Napoleon had 70,000 men and 300 guns, and his soldiers were no longer possessed of the spirit which inspired them when they crossed the Niemen. At this distance from France he had every reason to preserve the strength of his army as far as possible.

The enemy was in a position two and a half versts beyond Maloyaroslavetz. The French forces were distributed between that place and Mozhaisk. Davout's corps and two cavalry corps stood in front of Maloyaroslavetz; the Viceroy Eugene occupied the town and the valley of the Luzha; the Guard and two cavalry corps were between that place and Gorodnya; Ney with two divisions was between Gorodnya and Borovsk; Marchand's division behind that town; Poniatovski in Vereya; Mortier on the road from Kubinskoye to Vereya; Junot in Mozhaisk; the artillery park and baggage at Borovsk, Gorodnya, and between that place and Maloyaroslavetz.

On the morning of the 26th October Napoleon again rode towards Maloyaroslavetz with the Guard and two cavalry corps. He stopped at a bivouac fire short of the

Luzha River, and at nine o'clock received information that the Russians were retreating. They had left only a rearguard in front of Maloyaroslavetz to cover their retirement to Goncharovo.

Napoleon now decided to retreat to Mozhaisk and thence on Smolensk, although he was thus selecting a route that had been exhausted of supplies during the advance, when he might have marched by Medyn to Yukhnov and Yelnya. He had on the 24th written to Victor to send Gerard's division and a light cavalry brigade to meet the army by that route; he now changed the order, directing him to send by Vyazma and Dorogobuzh, with as many supplies as possible.

The Guard and two cavalry corps were now sent back to Borovsk, followed by Prince Eugene's corps; Davout, **Retreat** together with two cavalry corps, was left as rearguard. Ney, with all the baggage at Borovsk, was ordered to Vereya, to march next day to Mozhaisk; Poniatovski to take post at Yegoryevskoye, to cover the left flank of the army, and afterwards to march to Gzhatsk; Mortier was to hasten on from Vereya to Mozhaisk and Vyazma; Junot to move to Vyazma as soon as Mortier reached Mozhaisk. Davout was to march from Maloyaroslavetz with the rearguard at ten o'clock in the evening.

Napoleon's retreat had now begun in earnest. There

was to be no more manœuvring, but merely an effort to save the army.

Napoleon, having determined to march to Kaluga from Moscow, had two courses open to him. He might have attacked the Russians in their fortified position at Tarutino, and so cleared the way. Undoubtedly he chose the right course in retreating, rather than fight a doubtful battle. But when his plan had almost succeeded his irresolution led to failure. He still had it in his power to avoid a conflict and march by Medyn. But in the result we find him retreating by a route which he had better, as circumstances turned out, have taken in the first instance, thus saving time and, what was almost as important, the consumption of provisions. But it is not clear why he did not march on Medyn and Yelnya instead of taking his army by the exhausted and longer route through Mozhaisk. His troops were perhaps too scattered to follow the Russians immediately on the 26th. But he wasted the whole of the 25th when he might have been collecting his forces.

Kutuzov showed the usual tactics of the Russian in retiring unnecessarily from a strong position. He had advanced with timidity; he retreated with precipitation and in such confusion that Sir Robert Wilson, the British general attached to the Russian army, declared that the retreat resembled a rout.

CHAPTER XIII

THE RETREAT TO SMOLENSK

The March to Vyazma—Russian Movements—Napoleon at Vyazma—News from the Wings—Napoleon's Measures—Retreat continued—Kutuzov's Pursuit—Battle of Vyazma—Difficulties of the March—Kutuzov's Plans—Retreat to Smolensk—Ney's Rearguard—The Passage of the Vop—Russian Operations

NAPOLEON reached Vereya on the 27th October. There he found Poniatovski, who had arrived on the 23rd, and **The March to Vyazma** Mortier, who had marched from Moscow after blowing up the Kremlin, happily somewhat ineffectually. Mozhaisk was passed next day, and the battlefield of Borodino on the 29th. The field of battle still presented a frightful scene, strewn with corpses, fragments of uniform, arms, helmets and broken drums. Farther on was the Kolotzki monastery, turned into a hospital, where there were some 500 wounded, most of whom were taken on on carriages with the army, the Emperor even giving up his own vehicles for this purpose. Information had been given by a captured Russian officer that Kutuzov was marching direct on Smolensk, and the fact that the rearguard was followed only by Cossacks appeared to confirm this statement. Napoleon accordingly hurried on his march, fearing that the Russians would reach Vyazma or Smolensk by a shorter route.

Winter was now approaching, and although the nights were cold, the weather was fine and favourable. No snow had as yet fallen. Napoleon reached Vyazma on the 31st October, travelling in his carriage. On this day the French troops were disposed as follows :—the Old Guard and Murat's cavalry eight versts beyond Vyazma; Mortier and Junot—approaching Vyazma; the Viceroy and Poniatovski near Gzhatsk; Davout at Gridnevo, forming the rearguard, with orders to burn all villages and buildings as he passed.

During the march the cold gradually increased, and there were several degrees of frost at night. The demoralisation of the troops continued; the sick were constantly augmented; men cast off the burthen of their arms, and at every step were to be seen infantry soldiers without weapons and troopers without horses. Parties wandered off the road to seek for food and numbers found death. Discipline declined; famine conquered feelings of honour and subordination; soldiers no longer obeyed nor even respected their officers. Between Mozhaisk and Gzhatsk 400 out of 5700 Westphalians left the ranks. The baggage trains of various corps became mixed, and were plundered; and bloody strife took place between French soldiers and their allies.

Meanwhile Kutuzov was at first unaware of the French line of retreat; he thought they had taken the road from **Russian Movements** Maloyaroslavetz to Medyn. It was not until the 27th that the Russian army marched, when they followed the Medyn road to Polotnyanye Zavodi. The advanced guard under Miloradovich was directed on Nikolskoye, while Platov with his cavalry and Cossacks followed the main Smolensk road. Thus on the 1st November, when Napoleon's army was echeloned for a distance of ninety versts between Vyazma and Gridnevo, the Russians were following on their flanks and rear. Kutuzov's main forces were moving from Medyn to cut the French line of retreat at Vyazma; the advanced or now more properly flank guard of Miloradovich was in the interval between the main forces and the great Smolensk road, in the direction of Gzhatsk; Denisov's Cossacks were ahead of the advanced guard. Platov was following in the enemy's rear; and other Cossack detachments were making raids on the French flanks. A detachment under Count Ozharovski was directed on Yelnya and Smolensk to destroy the enemy's detachments and magazines. The corps which had been employed under Winzingerode, north of Moscow, now under General P. A. Kutuzov, was directed from Moscow on Gzhatsk, moving north of the Moskva River, to harass the right flank of the retreating army.

Napoleon halted on the 1st November at Vyazma,

remaining until midday of the 2nd. Here he received news from St Cyr of his evacuation of Polotzk ; from Victor of his movement from Smolensk to the Dwina ; and from the Duke of Bassano (Maret) from Vilna reporting the retirement of Schwarzenberg before Chichagov. From these reports he gathered that the Russians intended to cut his line of communications.

Napoleon at Vyazma

Wittgenstein had resumed the offensive and marched against St Cyr, who was in position before Polotzk, on the 15th October. The Russian general attacked on the 18th, driving the French into the town, and as Steinheil was advancing along the left bank of the Dwina from Disna, St Cyr evacuated Polotzk and withdrew across the Dwina, at the same time defeating Steinheil's advanced guard, and forcing that general to retreat to Disna. Wittgenstein then crossed the Dwina, and St Cyr retired on Chashniki, on the River Ula, where Victor effected a junction with him on the 29th October. Thus Smolensk, where Victor was to have formed a general reserve, and from whence he was to have advanced to meet the Grand Army or to support St Cyr or Schwarzenberg as occasion arose, was left with only a garrison.

News from the Wings

In the meantime, in the south-western theatre of operations Schwarzenberg had retreated before Chichagov's advance, and crossed the Bug at Drogichin, thus exposing the French line of retreat towards the Berezina. Chichagov remained near Brest-Litovsk until the 30th October, when he advanced towards Slonim, from whence, as will be seen, his march was continued to the Berezina.

Napoleon still hoped that he would be able to avoid the enemies closing in on every side. Victor and St Cyr should hold Wittgenstein in check, and Chichagov, marching by difficult roads through the Lithuanian forests, should be detained by Schwarzenberg's pursuit. Charpentier, governor of Smolensk, was directed to inform Victor that the Grand Army would be at Dorogobuzh on the 3rd November, and that the Emperor expected to receive there all information regarding the movements of the wings, and of the supplies and artillery available in Smolensk. He was to write to the Commandant at Vitebsk and the governor of Mohilev to prepare as much flour as possible for the army, and to inform them " that the movement of the army is voluntary, that it is a manœuvre to approach a hundred leagues nearer to the armies forming the wings; that, since leaving the environs of Moscow, we have no news of the enemy, with the exception of some Cossacks." Baraguay d'Hilliers, who was advancing from Smolensk by the Kaluga road to meet the Grand Army was directed to conform to the new movement. And Victor was informed that the object of the march was to bring the troops operating on the flanks into closer touch with the

Napoleon's Measures

Grand Army; and that in all probability the main forces, taking up a position between the Dwina and the Dnieper, would obtain touch with the corps under his command.

The French army, weakened by hunger, moved almost without a halt, with the exception of the troops that had **Retreat continued** reached Vyazma. Davout passed through Gzhatsk on the 1st November, and continued his march to get through the defile of Tzarevo-Zaimishchiye, harassed on the way by the Cossacks, and abandoning guns and waggons. He was followed immediately by Paskevich's division; and to the left of the main road marched the advanced guard of Miloradovich.

Miloradovich could not hope to cut off the whole French army from its advanced guard; there would be 38,000 men to oppose his and Platov's 25,000. But he intended to intercept the rearguard at Tzarevo-Zaimishchiye; his advanced troops came into touch with the French on the 1st November, but arrived too late to cut them off, as they passed through by night. On the 2nd the French army was situated as follows:— the Westphalians beyond Semlevo; Napoleon's headquarters and the Guard, with part of the reserve cavalry at Semlevo; Ney, who had orders to allow all the other troops to pass to form the new rearguard, at Vyazma; the Viceroy and Poniatovski, having passed some six versts beyond Fyoderovskoye, had halted to support Davout, who was close to that place. For want of cavalry the French were unable to obtain any information of the Russian movements.

Kutuzov reached Dubrova that day, preceded by an advanced guard under Raevski. Count Orlov-Denisov, with a flying column, made a raid on Vyazma and seized a gun and some prisoners. Platov, together with Paskevich's division, halted between Tzarevo-Zaimishchiye and Fyoderovskoye. Miloradovich, moving between Kutuzov and Platov, stopped at Spasskoye, a short march from Vyazma, on the night of the 2nd November. Next day Miloradovich and Platov arranged to attack the enemy; they were supported by two divisions of cuirassiers under Uvarov, while the main Russian army moved to Bikova, ten versts from Vyazma.

Kutuzov's Pursuit

Miloradovich began the attack on Davout with his cavalry on the morning of the 3rd November, when Ney was just south of Vyazma; the Viceroy Eugene and Poniatovski were nearing that place, and Davout, followed by Platov's Cossacks, was approaching Fyoderovskoye. But Davout, although weak in guns and cavalry, and suffering heavy loss, beat off his assailants and continued his retreat. At ten o'clock the Russian infantry came up, and attacked the French flank; Eugene had halted, and turned to assist Davout, while Ney was engaged south of Vyazma, and was later able to send back assistance. The Russian

Battle of Vyazma

attack was badly conducted, and although they inflicted heavy loss on their worn-out enemies, they suffered severely themselves. This running fight continued until evening, when, Davout's and Eugene's troops having passed through, Ney formed the rearguard and evacuated Vyazma, leaving the place in flames.

While both sides claimed the victory at Vyazma, the advantage remained with the French, who attained their object. Those terrible soldiers showed that their spirit and their martial qualities still held out, notwithstanding the privations they had undergone and the enemies who assailed them on every side. The result proved the soundness of Napoleon's dispositions in arranging for the relief of the rearguard at Vyazma. The French would probably have gained a considerable success had there been one officer in command to co-ordinate the disposition of the troops. But what is to be thought of the Russian Commander-in-Chief who, almost within the sound of the guns at Vyazma, where the invaders stood at bay, remained in inaction at Bikova ? It may be said that he knew the climate and the vicissitudes of the march would do the work without the expenditure of more troops, and that he left " a golden bridge " for his enemies. But the theory of the " golden bridge," so frequently and erroneously advanced, betrays a counsel of timidity, and Kutuzov here lost the opportunity of annihilating a great part of the Grand Army.

THE RETREAT TO SMOLENSK 185

Next day, when he arrived at Slavkovo, Napoleon heard of the action of Vyazma, which led him to halt until **Difficulties** the 5th. He even had an idea of forming **of the March** an ambush between Slavkovo and Dorogobuzh, to fall on the pursuers with all his troops, but this was soon abandoned. It had been getting colder, and the first snow fell on the 4th, adding to the miseries and the disorganisation of the army.

On the 5th headquarters and the Old Guard reached Dorogobuzh; the Westphalians, the Young Guard and the remains of the 2nd and 4th Cavalry Corps, passing through the town, were posted on the road to Smolensk; Poniatovski, the Viceroy and Davout between Slavkovo and Dorogobuzh; and Ney with the rearguard approached Slavkovo. Snow continued to fall, and frost increased. A large portion of the cavalry was lost and many carts and some guns were abandoned. When a horse fell, it was seized, cut to pieces and devoured.

Having no food and no proper clothing and boots, the French suffered terribly from cold, and marched with difficulty. There was an enormous number of stragglers, mostly unarmed. Ney wrote to Berthier on the 4th that "the roads were without exaggeration crowded by 4000 men of various regiments, who could not be induced to march together."

Physical suffering produced decline in *moral*; discipline vanished; everything gave way to the instinct of self-preservation. At night the sick and wounded wandered about the bivouacs, trying to secure a place at the fires. The mornings revealed the camping sites strewn with corpses, like fields of battle. The Russian bivouacs were constantly surrounded by crowds of unarmed French, to whom their enemies showed hospitality. They did not trouble to make these unfortunates prisoners, and many were slaughtered by the infuriated peasants. The survivors looked to Smolensk as towards a promised land. There they hoped to find everything they required, and to go into winter quarters.

Meanwhile Kutuzov continued his march by the parallel road to Yelnya; Miloradovich and Platov pursued the enemy from the rear and left flank. In order to cut the French off from the south, the Governors of Kaluga, Tula and other provinces were directed to send the militia levies to Roslavl, Mstislavl, Yelnya and other places. General Ertel was ordered with his detachment from Mozyr on Bobruisk. It was proposed to Chichagov to leave a corps of observation to watch Schwarzenberg, and to march to Minsk and Borisov; and to Wittgenstein to approach the Dnieper, leaving Steinheil to follow St Cyr, or to try and prevent the latter from joining Napoleon, should he make the attempt.

Kutuzov's Plans

On the 6th November Napoleon's headquarters reached Mikhalevka, where he heard that Victor had fought an action at Chashniki on the 2nd November, and had retreated to Syenno. At length the Emperor informed **Retreat to Smolensk** Victor of the perilous situation of the Grand Army, directed him to assume the offensive, attack the enemy, drive him across the Dwina, and occupy Polotzk; "on this depends the safety of the army," wrote Berthier. Here also Napoleon heard of the conspiracy of General Malet in Paris, a disturbing factor in the situation. He crossed the Dnieper on the 7th, and stopped near Solovyova. The army continued its retreat in the same order; but the Viceroy Eugene left the main road at Dorogobuzh, to march to Vitebsk by way of Dukhovshchina in order to open communications with the forces operating on the Dwina. The same day Baraguay d'Hilliers marched from Yelnya for Smolensk.

Napoleon entered Smolensk on the 9th November. There were 12 degrees (Réaumur) of frost, and an icy wind was blowing; the last march was accomplished on foot.

The weary march of the army continued. The road was strewn with dead men and horses, and the troops subsisted chiefly on the flesh of horses and dogs. The Cossacks continued to harass them on the march, although they did little but cut off stragglers. Between the 9th and 13th the army poured into Smolensk; but they were disappointed in their hopes of plenty. The magazines were besieged by crowds of famished men, unarmed, in rags and scarcely human in appearance, who seized whatever provisions they could lay hands on. On the night of the 9th the soldiers slaughtered two hundred horses for food, as there were no supplies of meat. Napoleon ordered the Guard to be furnished with supplies for fourteen days and the remainder of the army for six days.

During the retreat from Vyazma, Ney fought heroically with his rearguard. At Dorogobuzh he made a stand and drove back Miloradovich, who was in close pursuit, and set fire to the town before leaving it, but the snow prevented the flames from spreading, and the Russians halted there for the night.

<small>Ney's Rearguard</small>

Ney pressed on through a blinding snowstorm, and reached Smolensk on the evening of the 13th. From Dorogobuzh the pursuit relaxed, for Miloradovich turned off to the south-west to join the main army, and only light detachments followed the retreat. But still the rearguard had to fight in order to gain time at Smolensk, and when his disheartened soldiers threw down their arms Ney seized a musket and, himself setting the example, inspired them to renewed exertions.

It has already been related how the Viceroy Eugene had taken the road from Dorogobuzh to Vitebsk by way of Dukhovshchina. Napoleon had sent General Sanson with a party of officers and a small escort to survey the road and especially the River Vop. But this party was captured by the advanced guard of General P. A. Kutuzov, which had marched by a parallel route north of the main road and had reached Dukhovshchina.

Prince Eugene advanced from Dorogobuzh and crossed the Dnieper on the 7th November; the passage was difficult, and from twelve to sixteen horses had to be employed to drag each gun up the bank. As the march continued, men and horses died of hunger and cold, baggage was abandoned, and the corps was becoming disorganised when the bank of the Vop was reached on the 9th. Here a bridge, constructed the day before, was swept away by a flood, and the troops had to ford the river breast-high. The greater part of the artillery and baggage had to be abandoned, and, to make matters worse, Platov's Cossacks, who had followed from Dorogobuzh, attacked the rear. But Broussier's division, forming the rearguard, kept the Cossacks at bay, and covered the remainder of the force, which effected the passage by nightfall. The night was passed in open bivouac in the snow. Broussier's division crossed at dawn, leaving behind sixty-four guns, and the greater part of the baggage. There remained under arms not more than 6000 men. The march was continued to Dukhovshchina, followed by Platov, while from the town issued Ilovaiski's advanced guard of P. A. Kutuzov's detachment. Attacked in front and rear, the valiant remnant of the Viceroy's troops held their own, drove Ilovaiski from Dukhovshchina, and took possession of the town, which had been abandoned by its inhabitants. Here shelter and some food were found. Still pursued by Cossacks who cut off stragglers, but generally kept at a distance, the Viceroy entered Smolensk with the remains of his corps on the 13th November.

During this period Kutuzov had continued his march from Bikovo by Byeli-Kholm to Yelnya, where he **Russian Operations** arrived on the 8th November, and halted on the 9th. A flying column under Ozharovski, moving ahead of the army, passed Baltutino on the 8th, while Davidov's partisans were between Alexyeievo and the Yelnya road. These Cossacks, in conjunction with a detachment under Count Orlov-Denisov, next day attacked and eventually surrounded a brigade under General Augereau, forming Baraguay d'Hilliers' advanced guard, posted between Lyakhovo and Yazvino. After an obstinate resistance, in which many were killed and wounded, Augereau was obliged to surrender with over 1700 officers and men.

Kutuzov, meanwhile, had passed through Yelnya and reached Labkovo, on the Roslavl road on the 11th. On the 13th he crossed over to Shchelkanovo on the Mstislavl road. Miloradovich proceeded towards Chervonnoye with the advanced guard, where Orlov-Denisov, who was ahead, drove out a detachment of Poles. Ozharovski moved his detachment direct on Krasnoi; and P. A. Kutuzov marched to Dukhovshchina. Chichagov, having left a detachment of 25,000 men near Brest Litovsk to watch Schwarzenberg, was approaching Minsk. But Schwarzenberg recrossed the Bug, and marched towards Volkovisk, followed by Sacken, who commanded the Russian detachment. Schwarzenberg was not, however, in a position to co-operate with the Grand Army. He was based on Warsaw instead of, as he should have been, on Minsk. Wittgenstein was at Chashniki, where Victor, who was at Chereya, threatened him with a further advance.

Having assembled his forces at Smolensk, Napoleon decided to continue his retreat. Smolensk was untenable. His retreat on Orsha was threatened by Kutuzov, and Chichagov would soon be on the Berezina, while Wittgenstein menaced his other flank. Thus the only chance of escape was to lose no time in marching. Nor, as the supplies collected at Smolensk were exhausted, was there any object in staying at that place.

CHAPTER XIV

FROM SMOLENSK TO BORISOV

Retreat from Smolensk—Arrival at Krasnoi—Napoleon's Resolution — Battle of Krasnoi — Ney's Rearguard — From Krasnoi to Borisov—Action at Borisov—Chichagov's Movements—Disposition of Opposing Forces

NAPOLEON left Smolensk with the Guards by the Krasnoi road on the 14th November. Junot and the remnant of Poniatovski's corps had marched on the 12th. Eugene was to start next day, and Davout and Ney, whose corps still formed the rearguard, on the 15th.

Retreat from Smolensk

The army was reduced to some 50,000 men, calculated as follows :—

> Guard : infantry, 14,000 ; cavalry, 2000.
> 1st Infantry Corps, 10,000—Davout.
> 3rd Infantry Corps, 6000—Ney.
> 4th Infantry Corps, 5000—Prince Eugene.
> 5th Infantry Corps, 800—Poniatovski.
> 8th Infantry Corps, 700—Junot.
> Dismounted Cavalry, 500.
> Cavalry, 3000.
> Engineers and Artillery, 7000.

It is difficult to understand why Napoleon marched with his columns separated by such long intervals. Probably the want of good maps and of a knowledge of the roads prevented him from adopting a formation of parallel columns. He might, moreover, have marched along the north bank of the Dnieper to Orsha, thus having the river to protect his left flank.

The leading French column reached Krasnoi on the 14th, driving back Ozharovski's detachment, which had expelled the French garrison. The Emperor's headquarters with the guard remained that night at Koritnya.

<small>Arrival at Krasnoi</small>

On the Russian side, Kutuzov was at Volkovo, a detachment under Miloradovich at Knyaginino, and a detachment under Osterman attacked a French force (not specified but said to be Poles) near Kobizevo and took 6000 prisoners. This day there were 40 degrees of frost.

On the 15th the leading column passed Krasnoi and reached Liadi, while Napoleon caught up the Westphalians and entered Krasnoi with them. Miloradovich and Osterman reached the vicinity of the highroad near Rzhavka while Napoleon and the Guards were passing, but did no more than open a cannonade; some of the balls falling near the Emperor caused him to remark with indifference: "Bah! the bullets and shot have been flying about our legs these twenty years!"

Here, as ever, he displayed that cool disregard of personal danger which was one of his chief and most valuable characteristics. His courage was no less evident at Krasnoi than on the bridge of Arcola in 1797. On arrival at Krasnoi in the evening Napoleon heard of the presence of Ozharovski's detachment of six regiments with six guns at Kutkovo, and had them driven out with heavy loss by a night attack by a division of the Young Guard.

Hearing from prisoners that Kutuzov with the main Russian army was a short march distant from Krasnoi, **Napoleon's Resolution** the Emperor resolved to await the arrival from Smolensk of the other columns, in order to save them from being cut off. It was a great resolution, worthy of a great commander, to take such a risk in the immediate presence of an army 80,000 strong, with other armies of equal strength hurrying up on either flank to cut him off. He could have marched on to Orsha, leaving two-thirds of his army to almost certain destruction.

On the 16th November Eugene was waylaid on the road to Krasnoi by Miloradovich, who stood at Merlino. Rejecting a summons to surrender, the Viceroy fought his way bravely through these superior forces, and reached Krasnoi with the remains of his corps, amounting to 3000 men.

The situation of the Emperor now appeared sufficiently

desperate. Kutuzov was close by at Novoselki, and his advanced guard blocked the road by which Davout and Ney were approaching from Smolensk. An attack by the main Russian army, if carried through with vigour and resolution, must have a decisive effect. But Napoleon knew his enemy, and decided to take the offensive himself and clear the road for Davout. He accordingly made the following dispositions :—Mortier, with two divisions of the Young Guard, was to move out along the Smolensk road, followed by the Old Guard and thirty guns ; the Guard Cavalry and Latour-Maubourg were to form the reserve ; Claparède's division would hold Krasnoi. Eugene was to continue his march towards Orsha. Davout, having sent information as to the situation to Ney, set out from near Koritnya at three o'clock in the morning on the 17th November, with 7500 men and fifteen guns. At nine o'clock he was attacked by Miloradovich opposite Larionova, where the Russians had passed the night. But Miloradovich received orders from Kutuzov not to oppose Davout's march, but to content himself with attacking his rear, and the marshal reached Krasnoi with some loss. Meanwhile Napoleon **Battle of Krasnoi** had moved out at dawn and attacked the head of the Russian column at Uvarova, which enabled him to join hands with Davout, and no doubt relieved the pressure upon that officer. We have a fine picture of the Emperor ; calm in the hour of danger, "he stood on the frozen road, in his Polish cap of marten fur, and green velvet-lined fur coat with gold braid, leaning on a stick cut from a birch-tree," holding at bay 80,000 Russians more by the terror of his presence than by force of the feeble remains of the Grand Army that still held together under his command.

Kutuzov now extended his left, and ordered the greater part of his troops to turn Krasnoi by way of Sorokino on Dobroye. Napoleon, informed of this movement, decided to retreat, although this obliged him to abandon Ney with the rearguard. Kutuzov, becoming aware that the Emperor was present in person, stopped his movement, and the French retreated to Liadi.

Napoleon has been blamed for thus abandoning Ney, a course that has been falsely attributed to his desire for personal safety. But what useful purpose would have been served by his finding there, like the Emperor Julian, a glorious death? To remain in Krasnoi would have been the end of all things. Not only Ney's advanced guard, but the whole army must have been destroyed.

Ney left Smolensk at two A.M. on the 17th, with 6000 men and twelve guns; arriving near Krasnoi next afternoon, he found the road blocked by the whole Russian army. A lesser man would have surrendered. But this brave warrior had not come to the end either of his courage or resources. To a

Ney's Rearguard

summons to lay down his arms, he replied : " A marshal of France does not surrender ! "

His troops even captured some of the enemy's guns, although these were retaken. But it was impossible to make headway against the numbers which assailed him. The brave marshal now undertook one of the most wonderful marches recorded in history. With his forces greatly reduced he turned towards the Dnieper. Guided by an inaccurate map in an unknown country, he struck north to Sirokokoreniye, following a rivulet which he knew must flow into the river. He decided to pass the Dnieper and march along the right bank to Orsha. The pursuit had fortunately relaxed, the snow covered up his tracks, and a thaw followed on the frost. His only fear was that the melting of the ice would preclude the possibility of passage. The remnant of the rearguard came to the river near Gusinoye. A place was found where the ice would bear, and the soldiers crossed, abandoning guns and carts. Arrived on the far bank they turned towards Orsha, following a track scarcely discernible in the forest. And now a new danger presented itself. Platov's Cossacks had come from Smolensk and were taking the same route. They harassed the rearguard whenever they emerged into the open. Ney formed his men into a square, and marched on. The Cossacks opened fire with artillery, and Platov, thinking to complete the destruction of the enemy, directed his men to charge with the lance. But, inspired by their brave leader, the French kept their ranks, and fought their way to Yakubovo, where food and shelter were found on the night of the 19th. In the early morning of the 20th a Polish officer was sent to Orsha with news of the desperate situation of the rearguard. Napoleon had already left, thinking Ney lost, but Davout and the Viceroy Eugene were in the town. The latter at once marched out to Ney's assistance, met him on the road, and conducted him in safety to Orsha. Well might Napoleon exclaim when hearing that evening of his safety: "He is the bravest of the brave." His rearguard was reduced to 900 men.

The events round Krasnoi reduced the strength of the Grand Army by some 25,000 men. But that any had escaped is remarkable, and to be ascribed, apart from the bold measures of the Emperor, to the timidity and inaction of the Russian Commander-in-Chief. But it has been recorded that Kutuzov said to Sir Robert Wilson, who was in his camp: "I do not consider that the destruction of Napoleon's power would be advantageous to Europe; it would lead to the supremacy of England instead of the supremacy of France." That aspect of the question, however, had nothing to do with the duties of the general commanding in the field.

After evacuating Krasnoi, Napoleon passed the night at Liadi, and took the road to Orsha before dawn on the

19th November. There was a thaw after the hard frost, making the road very heavy, and Napoleon left his carriage and marched on foot to encourage the troops. He reached Dubrovna in the afternoon, and established himself there in the house of the Princess Liubomirskaya. Davout with his corps and Mortier with the Young Guard formed the rearguard. Zaionchek, who had succeeded to Poniatovski's command, owing to the latter's illness, and Junot reached Orsha this day, the Viceroy Eugene being between Dubrovna and Orsha. There was less difficulty about supplies, as the inhabitants of the Mohilev Government had not left their villages. The army was now reduced to 25,000 men, with little cavalry or artillery.

From Krasnoi to Borisov

In Dubrovna the Emperor received news of the Russian occupation of Vitebsk, of an unsuccessful action fought by Victor at Chashniki on the 14th November, and of the occupation of Minsk by Chichagov on the 16th. He sent orders to Dombrovski[1] to collect his troops at Borisov and defend the bridge-head at that town; to Bronikovski, governor of Minsk, to join Dombrovski and headquarters at Borisov; to Oudinot to march immediately to Borisov, collect the troops there, and together with his corps move on Minsk as the advanced guard of the army; intending to gain possession of that town and establish himself behind the Berezina. Victor was directed to protect

[1] Dombrovski had been with his division at Bobruisk.

Borisov, Vilna and Orsha, so that when the army was established at Minsk he could move to the Upper Berezina, cover the Vilna road and join St Cyr, then retiring on Lithuania. Next day Napoleon reached Orsha and took up his quarters in the Jesuit monastery. Orders were sent to Victor to be prepared to be at Borisov on the 25th or 26th to form the rearguard of the army.

At Orsha Napoleon reorganised the remains of his army, finding there some small arms, thirty-six guns, and other supplies.

Still in the hope of forestalling Chichagov on the Berezina, the march was continued next day to Kokhanov and on the 22nd to Tolochin. The previous day Chichagov had forced Dombrovski out of Borisov, and occupied that place with his 34,000 men, the Pole falling back to Bobr, which was reached the same day by Oudinot with 8000 men. Victor was at Chereya with 11,000.

On the Russian side—Kutuzov, after detaching a strong force under Yermolov in pursuit of Napoleon, was at Lanniki on the 21st, awaiting the crossing of the Dnieper by his advanced guard under Miloradovich at Kopis. Wittgenstein was at Chashniki with 30,000 men; Sacken, with 25,000 had retreated to Shereshovo before Schwarzenberg, who had advanced to Radetzko with 35,000 men. P. A. Kutuzov had reached Babinovichy.

Rain fell for some days from the 20th, making the

marching still more difficult. At Tolochin Napoleon heard of the capture of Borisov by Chichagov, and realised that the only course now remaining was to force the passage of the Berezina in the face of a Russian army. The possibility of taking a direct route north of Borisov on Molodechno, crossing the Berezina where fordable, proposed by Jomini, was rejected on account of the strong position of Wittgenstein at Chashniki ; while other Russian forces, moving by shorter routes, might forestall him at Vilna.

Napoleon's initial plans for the passage of the Berezina were as follows :—Oudinot was to occupy the ford at Veselovo, construct bridges there, and cover them by fortifications ; Victor—to hold the Lepel road in order to cover Oudinot from Wittgenstein. At four-thirty in the morning of the 24th orders were given to the chief of pioneers, General Eblé, and of engineers, General Chasseloup, to join Oudinot at Borisov, and proceed with the construction of the bridges over the Berezina. Pontoons, sappers and miners were ordered to Borisov. The order was given for half the carts and waggons to be burnt.

Meanwhile Oudinot met with and defeated Chichagov's advanced guard at Loshnitzi, and on the French advance **Action at Borisov** being continued the Russian commander withdrew to the other bank of the river, occupied the bridge-head and destroyed the bridge at Borisov. Oudinot occupied the town and reconnoitred the river for a point of passage on the 24th. This was found at Studyanka; a feint was to be made at Mali Stakhov. In driving the Russians out of Borisov, Oudinot took a great part of their baggage and killed or captured a thousand men, exclusive of the sick and wounded who were all abandoned in the town.

While these events were taking place, Wittgenstein was pursuing Victor on his retreat from Chereya. The French marshal retired fighting on Bobr, where he arrived on the 24th, thus leaving open to Wittgenstein the direct route to Studyanka. Victor reached Loshnitza on the 25th, the day on which Napoleon had assembled all his other forces at Borisov.

Chichagov, posted at the bridge-head opposite Borisov, was misled by movements of French parties to believe that the passage of the Berezina was to be attempted below that place. Accordingly, leaving a part of his force at the bridge-head, he marched down the river to Shabashevichy, on the 25th, the day on which Oudinot moved up to Studyanka. Chichagov had posted a detachment under Chaplitz at Brili, opposite Studyanka, but that officer received orders to withdraw to the bridge-head, which he did, although he observed and had information of the preparations on the opposite bank of the river. He, however, left some Cossack posts along the bank. On this day also Napoleon entered Borisov, riding part of the way, but at times being

Chichagov's Movements

forced by the cold, as frost had again set in, to proceed on foot.

Thus on the evening of the 25th November, when Oudinot set out for Studyanka, Napoleon's main strength was partly at Borisov, where was the Guard and Junot and Ney, to whose corps had been added the remains of Dombrovski's detachment, Poniatovski's corps and the Mohilev garrison; part on the march near Loshnitza; Victor's corps north of the main road, at Ratulichy, to cover the army from Wittgenstein. On the Russian side—Chichagov was between Borisov and Shabashevichy, with a detachment at Usha under O'Rorke, who had sent his cavalry to Nizhnoye Berezino; Wittgenstein was at Baran, his advanced guard under Albrecht at Yanchina, *en route* to Borisov. Platov, following the French rear, was at Nachi; Ermolov was at Malyavka; Miloradovich was at Tolochin; Ozharovski had seized the French magazines at Mohilev; Kutuzov, with his main army, stood at Kopis.

Disposition of Opposing Forces

The situation which Napoleon had to face was sufficiently appalling to daunt the stoutest heart. Pressed in rear and on both flanks, he found himself arrested in front by a river difficult to pass and defended by an entire army. With soldiers half-dead with cold and hunger he had to overcome obstacles which might have arrested the best organised army. A thaw had melted the ice of the Berezina, and the river which would have been passable a few days before was now pouring in an ice-laden flood between its banks. Now it was necessary to construct bridges, a difficult work in such a stream. The forces brought from Moscow did not exceed 20,000 men; the corps of Victor and Oudinot amounted to as many. These were encumbered by some 50,000 unarmed men and followers. To these were opposed Chichagov's 30,000; on the right Wittgenstein and Steinheil's 25,000; and Kutuzov's 80,000 were approaching from the left and rear.

CHAPTER XV

THE PASSAGE OF THE BEREZINA

The Point of Passage—Construction of Bridges—26th November—27th November—Capture of a French Division—Passage continued—Battle of the Berezina—Repulse of Russians on both Banks—Comments—Napoleon on the Berezina

NAPOLEON left Borisov on the 25th November and established his headquarters at Stari Borisov, from whence he rode over to Studyanka at dawn next day.

The village of Studyanka stands on the slope of the left bank of the Berezina, a hundred and fifty paces from the river. The heights on that side dominate the right bank, where marshes, frozen since the 24th, favoured the movement of troops under cover of batteries established at Studyanka. The crest of the high ground extending along the left bank of the Berezina covers the road leading from the town of Borisov, in front of Stari Borisov, and farther through the village of Bitchi to Studyanka. On the right bank of the river runs the main country road leading from Bobruisk, in front of the Borisov bridge-head, and farther to Bolshoi Stakhov and the Stakhov forest; after passing through the forest and leaving Brili on the right, the road turns almost at right angles at a distance of four versts from that village, and passes through great forests and difficult defiles formed by the River Gaina to Zembin and Molodechno, where it joins the main road to Vilna.

When Napoleon arrived at Studyanka, the hard frost had frozen the broad marshes lying along the Berezina, but the river was not yet frozen, and was covered with large blocks of ice which rendered difficult the construction of the bridges. At eight o'clock in the morning General Corbinot was sent across with a squadron, and when materials had been collected some rafts to carry ten men each were constructed and 400 of Dombrovski's riflemen followed. At the same time all Oudinot's artillery, 40 guns, was posted on the heights at Studyanka.

The detachment that had crossed over soon drove back into the forest the posts left by Chaplitz at Brili, and the construction of two bridges was begun, one about a hundred yards distant from the other, that on the right being intended for the passage of troops, and the one on the left for artillery and waggons. The wood for the bridges was taken from the houses in Studyanka, the iron parts were brought from Orsha by General Eblé, who undertook the construction of the bridges. Great difficulties were met with. The river had risen until it was a hundred yards in width, and it was six feet deep in some places.

Working under the eye of the Emperor, the brave sappers stood in water up to their shoulders, and constructed the bridges as rapidly as possible, braving death, and losing half their number. The right-hand bridge was ready by eleven o'clock, when Oudinot and Dombrovski crossed with their troops, together with Dumerc's cuirassier division. These troops passed in front of the Emperor in perfect order, with shouts of *Vive l'Empereur*! Two guns were also despatched to the other side.

In the meantime Chaplitz had returned towards Brili, but satisfied himself with the occupation of the edge of the forest; he was driven back on Stakhov by Oudinot. French detachments were sent towards Zembin, where they occupied the bridges and viaducts across the marshes of the River Gaina, the Cossacks there retreating on Stakhov, thus opening the road to Vilna.

The second bridge was ready at four in the afternoon; some guns were taken across, but the bridge broke down and took some hours to repair.

Meanwhile the debris of the army was approaching Studyanka. Ney arrived when Oudinot had crossed the river, and Claparede followed; the Guard was there; Victor alone was far in rear; leaving Ratulichi on the morning of the 26th, he relieved Davout at Loshchina with a rearguard under Partouneaux and Delaitre's brigade of cavalry, and entered Borisov in the night;

the remains of the corps of the Viceroy, Davout and Junot were approaching Borisov.

During the 26th Chichagov had remained at Shabashevichy, and it was not until late in the day that one of his detachments discovered that Napoleon had gone to Studyanka and was there passing the river. This information was sent to Kutuzov at Kopis. Wittgenstein was now moving from Zhiskovo on Kostritza, and the same day Platov approached Loshnitza, Yermolov reached Krupki, and Miloradovich was at Malyavka.

26th November

During the night the bridge intended for wheeled vehicles broke down twice, becoming useless from eight o'clock until eleven o'clock, and from two o'clock until six in the morning of the 27th. This led to extensive crowding on the left bank of the Berezina. In order to maintain order as far as possible and hasten the crossing, Napoleon himself passed the night of the 26th in a hut near the bridges; when he rested, his place was taken by Murat, Berthier or Lauriston. Ney's troops and the Young Guard crossed during the night. Every effort was made to get the unarmed men and followers across, but most of these preferred to wander round Borisov in search of food.

On the morning of the 27th Victor's corps came up, with the exception of Partouneaux's division left as rearguard at Borisov. The arrival of Victor ensured the crossing being covered from Wittgenstein, so at one o'clock in the afternoon Napoleon sent the Old Guard over and rode across himself. The Baden brigade and the artillery of Daendels' division followed; then the remains of the corps of the Viceroy, Davout and Junot. Thus there remained at Studyanka only Girard's division and one of Daendels' brigades, Fournier's cavalry division and the reserve artillery of the 9th Corps; Partouneaux's division and Delaitre's cavalry were holding Borisov.

27th November

As the troops crossed to the other bank, they formed front in order of battle towards the Stakhov forest. But the Russians feared to attack, and throughout the day the opposing forces stood face to face within musket-shot. A reinforcement reached Chaplitz in the evening, but the Russians appeared to be paralysed by the presence of Napoleon. Had they attacked with vigour, they must have rendered the position of the French most desperate. The larger bridge broke down again at four o'clock, and was not repaired before six. The sick, the wounded and the stragglers crowded the entrance to the bridges, and together with horses and carts filled the whole space between Studyanka and the bank of the river. Victor alone, with 6000 men, held the heights above on the left bank of the Berezina, while Partouneaux was still in Borisov, to draw off the attention of Wittgenstein and to hold back Chichagov at the broken bridge, whither the latter had returned from Usha.

Partouneaux repelled at Borisov an attempt by Chichagov's troops to cross from the bridge-head. He then started for Studyanka, but at three o'clock in the afternoon of the 27th he was cut off by Wittgenstein's advanced guard, which had reached Stari Borisov, his march being impeded by baggage carts and thousands of unarmed stragglers who crowded round his columns. Partouneaux bravely attempted to cut his way through, but the odds were too great, and he was forced to retire to Borisov, where he was soon surrounded by the advancing Russians. Still this brave Frenchman would not surrender. At night he broke out again, and attacked Wittgenstein's army, obtaining some success near Stari Borisov, but at length, surrounded on every side, he was forced to surrender. Next morning Delaitre, who had retreated again to Borisov with his cavalry, was also obliged to surrender. The captured included 5 general officers, 7000 men and 3 guns. One battalion, 120 strong, managed to escape along the bank of the Berezina and joined Victor. This was the only signal success obtained by the Russian arms during the entire campaign.

Capture of a French Division

Meanwhile Chichagov had thrown a pontoon bridge over the river at Borisov, and entered into communication with Wittgenstein and Platov, who had arrived there. Chichagov informed Wittgenstein that he would attack the enemy next day, the 28th November, and asked for some reinforcements, as, he said, "the enemy is in all probability four times as strong as the army of the Danube." Wittgenstein said he would co-operate on the left bank, and sent Platov and Yermolov across to support Chichagov.

During the night of the 27th the French continued to pass artillery and baggage over the river. Some troops were sent on through Zembin, taking as much baggage and as many sick, wounded and unarmed men as possible, to join Wrede's corps at Vileika, guard the passage of the Vilia, and obtain supplies for the army. Napoleon, intending to preserve the bridges until the 29th, reinforced Victor, who disposed 8000 men and 14 guns on the plateau behind the stream running into the Berezina immediately below Studyanka. These troops were skilfully posted, the infantry being mostly withdrawn behind the crest, which was occupied only by a line of sharpshooters; the guns, on the left, commanded the approaches, while some artillery on the other side of the Berezina flanked the position; the few cavalry, amounting to some 300 men under Fournier, were in rear of the left.

Passage continued

Battle of the Berezina

On the 28th Wittgenstein's advanced guard drove in Victor's advanced posts from the village of Bitchi in the early morning, and at eight o'clock established themselves on the high ground facing the French. Russian reinforcements continually arrived, and a force was sent round to turn Victor's left, whilst at the same time guns opened on his right and on the bridges and masses collected on the left bank near the point of crossing.

These people—the sick, the wounded, the followers, including women and children, and the thousands of unarmed stragglers who had been wandering from camp fire to camp fire like gaunt spectres during the retreat—rushed in tumultuous masses towards the bridges, mixed up with horses and vehicles. Ségur describes the scene that ensued : " About midday the first shot from the enemy's batteries fell amid this chaotic mass. Then, as in all extreme circumstances, men's hearts were laid bare, and acts of the lowest infamy and of the sublimest heroism were exhibited. Some, with relentless fury, cut themselves a dreadful passage, sword in hand. Others forced a still more cruel way with their carriages. They drove them mercilessly over the crowd of wretched beings whom they crushed in their course. With atrocious avarice they sacrificed their companions in misfortune to the preservation of their baggage." Hundreds were crushed on the bridges, and thousands perished in the ice-laden torrent that flowed below.

" To complete the confusion and horror the bridge for the artillery cracked and broke. The column which was in the act of crossing this narrow passage tried in vain to retreat. The crowd which pressed on from behind, unconscious of the disaster, and deaf to the cries of those

THE PASSAGE OF THE BEREZINA

before them, pushed forward and precipitated them into the chasm into which they were soon thrown in their turn."

"The whole stream was at length diverted to the other bridge. A number of large caissons, heavy carriages, and field-pieces flocked to it from all parts. Urged on by their drivers and carried rapidly down a frozen and rugged declivity, through the thick of this mass of human beings, they crushed the unfortunate wretches who happened to be caught between them; then, meeting with a heavy shock, most of them were overturned with violence and knocked down all around them in their fall. Whole ranks of men driven in desperate terror by these conflicting obstacles got entangled with them, were thrown down and crushed by other ranks who rushed on to the same fate in frightful and ceaseless succession."

The same horrible struggle ensued at the other bridge.

"Amid the fearful din made by the roar of a furious hurricane, the thunder of artillery, the whistling of the tempestuous wind, the hissing of bullets, the bursting of shells, the shouts, groans, and frightful imprecations of fierce and despairing men, this tumultuous mass heard not the wailings of the victims over whom it rolled."

During the progress of this scene, the battle for the protection of the passage had waged fiercely on the heights above. The French cavalry beat back the attack on

Victor's left, and a fierce counter-attack on the Russian centre confirmed this success. The Russian reserves came up and arrested the advance of the French who had broken through their centre, while a fresh attack on his left obliged Victor to throw back that wing to cover Studyanka and the approaches to the bridges. Still the French fought until dark against the great odds brought against them. The combat ceased after dark, and during the night Victor withdrew across the Berezina, leaving a small rearguard to cover the retreat of the remaining stragglers and baggage. He had lost half his force, but had inflicted great losses on the enemy, and had held his own throughout the day with remarkable skill and valour.

Meanwhile on the right bank of the Berezina Chichagov had advanced from Stakhov at dawn to attack the French who had crossed over. There Ney and Oudinot with 8000 men, including 1500 cavalry, stood with their right towards the thick forest traversed by the Borisov road. Oudinot occupied the right and centre, and Ney the left wing of the position, which was about two versts in extent. In reserve stood the guard, 4000 strong, under the personal leadership of Napoleon.

The Russian attack was badly carried out, and was preceded by the assumption of the offensive by Ney, who drove back the enemy's advanced guard. Oudinot was wounded early in the engagement, and Ney then assumed

THE PASSAGE OF THE BEREZINA 215

command of the whole line. A charge of the French cavalry under Dumerc resulted in great havoc and the capture of 1500 prisoners. Russian reinforcements then poured in, and the battle continued with unabated fury until nightfall, but the Russians were unable to gain a footing beyond Stakhov.

Thus the remnant of Napoleon's Grand Army held its own against this combined attack on both banks of the Berezina. In the words of Ségur, " Above sixty thousand men, well fed, well clothed, and completely unarmed, attacked eighteen thousand half-naked, ill-armed, famished men separated by a river, surrounded by morasses, and encumbered by more than fifty thousand stragglers, sick and wounded, and by an enormous mass of baggage. For two days the cold and misery were so intense that the Old Guard lost a third and the Young Guard one half of their effective men." On the right bank Ney had driven the Russians back on Stakhov, and on the left Victor held the plateau of Studyanka and protected the bridges from Russian bayonets although he could not cover them from artillery fire. Victor's rearguard retired across the river in the early morning of the 29th November, and at half-past eight the bridges were set on fire in rear of the retreating army.

Repulse of Russians on both Banks

The losses of the Grand Army on the Berezina amounted probably to not less than 20,000 men, or about half the number that had reached the river under arms; and in addition not less than 20,000 unarmed stragglers were captured or perished.

Kutuzov with the main Russian army had crossed the Dnieper at Kopis on the 26th November. On the 29th he halted short of the Berezina, which he intended to cross at Zhukovetz, and some forty versts south-east of Borisov. Thus he found himself far from the decisive point at the decisive moment.

It was not only the absence of his army, but the want of unity of command which it entailed that led to the Russian failure on the Berezina. There were in the neighbourhood ample troops to have completed the destruction of the Grand Army, had their movements been methodically co-ordinated from the beginning. As it was, but for the loss of Partouneaux's division, the French operations were wonderfully successful, and the passage of the Berezina again proved the genius of the great commander, the skill and fortitude of his marshals and the valour of his troops.

Comments

It is, however, only fair to the Russians to point out that they were not aware of the disorganised and famished condition of their opponents, while the presence of some 50,000 unarmed men increased the appearance of strength of the army when viewed from a distance. Thus Chichagov supposed that Napoleon was still at the head of 80,000 men when he arrived on the Berezina, and the moral effect of the Emperor's presence was equivalent to another 80,000.

Jomini points out that, with regard to Kutuzov's circumspection, it was most important for him to preserve the precious nucleus of his army, as the ulterior situation must in the event be influenced by political considerations; and it was essential to Russia "to be in a position to decide Prussia and Austria to detach themselves from the French alliance, or to resist them if they remained faithful to it."

It may be said, on the other hand, that the destruction of the remainder of the Grand Army and the capture of the person of the French Emperor would have placed Russia in the strongest position both with regard to power and prestige to dictate terms to Europe, and a consideration of this factor seems to nullify the opinion of Jomini. Surely both political and military considerations should have dictated the advisability of terminating at one stroke by concentration of effort and resolution in execution, the existence of the Grand Army and the power of Napoleon.

The passage of the Berezina where, says Ségur, Napoleon succeeded in saving 60,000 out of 80,000 men, was accomplished mainly by the presence and the dispositions of the Emperor himself.

Napoleon on the Berezina

" He stayed up to the last moment on these dismal banks, near the ruins of Brili, without shelter, and at the head of his Guard, a third part of whom had been destroyed by the storm . . . at night they bivouacked in a square around their chief. . . . During these three days and nights, Napoleon, whose eye and whose thoughts appeared to wander from the midst of the faithful band in three directions at once, supported the second corps by his presence and by his orders, defended the ninth and the passage across the river by his artillery, and united his exertions to those of Eblé in saving as much as possible from the general wreck. Lastly he directed the march of the remnant of his army, in person, towards Zembin, whither Prince Eugene had preceded him."

CHAPTER XVI

FROM THE BEREZINA TO THE NIEMEN

Retreat from the Berezina—Napoleon leaves the Army—The Army reaches Vilna—Passage of the Niemen—Ney's Last Stand—Macdonald's Retreat—Schwarzenberg's Retirement

Retreat from the Berezina

NAPOLEON left the Berezina at six o'clock in the morning of the 29th November, and drove through Zembin to Kamen, where he remained for the night with his Guard. The Viceroy and Davout reached Pleshchenitza; Victor stopped at Zembin; and Ney occupied a position short of that place on the same date. Only the forethought of Napoleon in sending on a force to open up the communications through this marshy country assured the safe retreat of the army.

On the Russian side Chichagov had sent a detachment towards Pleshchenitza on the 28th, and next day followed the retreating enemy, who had burnt the bridges behind them. The detachment nearly captured Oudinot at Pleshchenitza, having dispersed his escort, but the Marshal with seventeen men defended himself in a house, and held out until relieved by the arrival of two Westphalian battalions. Platov and Wittgenstein took up the pursuit by lines to the left and right of Chichagov respectively. Kutuzov himself moved slowly, and had not reached the Berezina on the 29th. He intended to direct his further advance across the Berezina at Zhukovetz, and thence through Smolevichy and Volozhin on Noviya Troki. Other detachments were to conform to the general movement.

Napoleon, still hoping to halt his troops for a time on the road to Vilna, for reorganisation and rest, had directed Wrede, who was at Dokshitzi with the remains of the Bavarian corps, to move to Vileika to cover the crossing of the Vilia, collect supplies for the army, and open communication with the commandant of Smorgoni, who had been directed to provision the magazines in Smorgoni and Oshmiani. Supplies were to be sent to meet the retreating army, and the remaining cattle despatched to Vilna so that they should not fall into the hands of the Cossacks.

But in a few days the army had practically ceased to exist. Few men remained in the ranks; but on the 4th December Ney made a fine stand with the rearguard at the entrance to Molodechno, and, with the aid of the remains of Victor's corps, drove off Chichagov's advanced guard.

The Emperor now decided to leave the army, where his presence could no longer be of any use, but might even be a source of embarrassment. On the 4th December Victor wrote to the Chief-of-the-Staff: "The

FROM THE BEREZINA TO THE NIEMEN 221

action which the rearguard has fought is the last effort that it can make against our enemies; the troops which compose it are to-day so reduced and the few that remain so miserable, that I am obliged to avoid every species of engagement. The enemy's vedettes and ours are in sight of one another; I shall in all probability be followed to-day as persistently as yesterday, and I think it would be convenient for his Majesty to keep at a greater distance from us."

Napoleon leaves the Army

Napoleon set out from Smorgoni on the 5th December, after handing over the command to Murat, and drove straight through to Vilna. As he himself said to Maret: "The army no longer exists; a disorganised crowd, wandering in search of food and shelter, cannot be called an army."

At dawn on the 8th December the Emperor crossed the Russian frontier at Kovno, where he had arrived less than six months earlier at the head of 400,000 men. Two days later he reached Warsaw, and on the 19th December he arrived in Paris, two days after the appearance there of the famous 29th Bulletin, in which he announced the disastrous conclusion of his invasion of Russia.

Napoleon has been blamed for leaving his army. But of what use was it for him to remain with the shattered remnant of his troops, to share their fate, to pass with them beneath "the Caudine Forks"? Had he been only a general, the matter would have been different.

But he was the ruler of a great Empire, at the western end of which the army of his most persistent enemies was contending for the mastery of the Peninsula. In Paris his presence was necessary to strengthen and even to secure his Government. Between him and France stretched 600 leagues of territory inhabited by peoples and ruled by monarchs whom he had humbled, ready on the first opportunity to rise against the Emperor of the West. Who but he would be able to gather together in four months a new army of 300,000 men and 600 guns with which to appear, once more terrible in battle, on the fields of Lutzen, Bautzen and Leipzig?

Meanwhile the debris of the Grand Army continued on its woeful way. The frost increased in intensity. In the three marches between Smorgoni and Vilna more than 20,000 men succumbed. The remainder, half dead with cold and hunger, a famished crowd, burst into Vilna on the 9th December. Provisions were ample, but the disorder was so great that they could not be distributed and the magazines had to be given up to pillage. Wittgenstein and Chichagov followed close upon their heels, but with greatly reduced forces. The former had only 15,000 men remaining. Ney, a rearguard in himself, held off the enemy where possible with incomparable valour.

The Army reaches Vilna

At length the Niemen was reached at Kovno, and, covered by Ney with a rearguard of 700 men, the shattered remnant of the mighty host that had crossed the river six months before in all the brave panoply of war, fled across the ice into the allied country that lay beyond. There were a thousand infantry and cavalry still armed, nine guns, and about 20,000 stragglers covered with rags, many of them wounded and frost-bitten. As many had remained behind in Vilna.

Passage of the Niemen

On the 14th December Ney made his last stand at Kovno with the small garrison which he found there. He checked the Russian advance for a time. "He then," says Ségur, "passed through Kovno and over the Niemen, fighting the whole of the way, never hastening into flight, always the last in the march, supporting to the very last moment the honour of our arms, and for the hundredth time in the course of forty days and forty nights, ready to sacrifice his own life and liberty to save a few more Frenchmen from the dreadful wreck. He at length quitted that fatal country, the last man of the Grand Army to leave it, proving to the world that even Fortune herself is powerless against the energy of true valour, and that the genuine hero converts everything into glory, even the most serious and accumulated disasters. He reached the allied bank at eight o'clock at night."

Ney's Last Stand

Except for this example of the valour of one man, the retreat after the passage of the Berezina had been accomplished presents nothing that is of military interest. Murat reached Konigsberg with a thousand men, followed by a few thousand stragglers.

Macdonald's operations round Riga had come to a standstill, and it was not until the 18th December that **Macdonald's** he received news of the events that had taken **Retreat** place, and orders to retire on Tilsit, where he arrived on the 28th. There he was deserted by the Prussians under Yorck, who on the 30th December concluded a convention with the Russians under the terms of which he agreed to remain neutral for two months. Thus with his corps reduced to 9000 men, Macdonald continued his march to Konigsberg.

It has been related that Schwarzenberg had advanced towards Minsk. On the 14th December he withdrew **Schwarzen-** from Slonim to Byelostok, and a week later **berg's** concluded an armistice, taking up a position **Retirement** to cover Warsaw, from which he did not retire until the end of January 1813.

CHAPTER XVII

THE CAUSES OF FAILURE

THE failure of Napoleon's campaign of 1812 has been frequently and indeed generally ascribed to the early and excessive cold of the climate. Thus even the historian of the Peninsular War says that "when winter came only four days sooner than he expected, the giant's scheme became a theme for children's laughter!" It is, however, a fact that the cold was neither earlier nor more severe than usual. Hard frosts did not set in until the 5th November; there was a thaw for some days prior to the passage of the Berezina, and the cold did not become extreme until after that event. The rigours of the climate were no greater than in the campaign of Eylau, but in the latter there was no want of provisions, of transport, and of shelter, and the army did not become disorganised.

The primary cause of failure is expressed in Montaigne's maxim: "Great and distant enterprises perish from the very magnitude of the preparations made to ensure their success." The vastness of the distances, the numbers of the army bringing in its train difficulties of supply and transport requisite for its maintenance, the long-drawn-out line of communications—these combined to render success unattainable. Napoleon undertook the impossible; not even his genius could overcome the difficulties encountered, or find a remedy for the "strategic consumption" of his army inseparable from the ever-lengthening line of communications from the Vistula to Moscow.

Viewing Europe as a whole, we find the French Emperor engaged in war in two directions, both east and west, which rendered concentration of effort impossible.

Many causes of failure have already been indicated in these pages. They may conveniently be recapitulated. Unforeseen factors, the Turkish peace and the Swedish alliance, influenced the situation after the opening of the campaign. Political errors and omissions were the cause of these disadvantages, and if they were not expected and provided for, as appears to have been the case, the campaign should not have been undertaken without measures to meet them. They resulted in the freedom of two armies to operate on the flanks of the advance.

The Grand Army was half composed of foreigners; and as a consequence neither a high standard of discipline nor whole-hearted devotion could be expected. Disorder manifested itself as soon as Russian territory was entered. People of twenty nations might gain victory under such a leader, but were bound to lose cohesion and discipline under the vicissitudes of failure. This polyglot composition was a primary cause of a great army dissolving into bands of marauders.

Immense difficulties of supply and transport were met with. Depots were established at too great a distance from the army, at Dantzig and Konigsberg. The roads and rivers were covered with supplies, but they could not be brought up to the troops. The country provided little, and the want of forage in particular led to immense loss in transport animals and cattle, as well as in cavalry and artillery horses.

It has been said by some writers that the campaign might have opened six weeks earlier, but it was necessary to wait for grazing for the animals, which would not have been sooner available. Moreover, as it was, Napoleon had ample time to retreat before winter set in, had he not lingered in Moscow; so this cannot be indicated as a cause of failure.

The Emperor lingered too long in Vilna, and it certainly seems that the junction of Barclay and Bagration at Smolensk should have been prevented by the destruction of one or the other. The golden moment for vigorous and resolute action against one of the enemy's separated wings was lost. Bagration escaped when he should have been crushed, and full advantage was not taken of the Russian strategical error in retiring on the Drissa camp.

A swift advance might have thrown Barclay back upon the Baltic.

The fine turning movement that brought the Grand Army to Smolensk failed to produce the results expected for reasons that have been detailed. Napoleon might have contented himself with the occupation of the line of the Dnieper in 1812, and deferred a further advance until the following spring. He had considered this plan; but it was impossible to subsist the army in a depopulated and devastated country. He had either to advance or retrace his steps; his prestige throughout Europe and the necessity of its maintenance rendered it impossible for him to acknowledge failure by a retrograde movement. Lithuania afforded no resources, all supplies having already been requisitioned by the Russians.

There was no general rising of the Poles such as had been anticipated, as Napoleon did not fulfil their expectations. But he had to consider that the re-establishment of a kingdom of Poland would in all probability have alienated Austria, whose co-operation, or at least neutrality, was indispensable to him during this campaign.

The troops of Macdonald, Oudinot, St Cyr and Victor on the line of communications should have been under one commander. They might then have crushed Wittgenstein and have been of more assistance in the retreat.

Napoleon had hoped for a decisive battle west of the Dwina. In this hope he was disappointed by the continued retreat of the Russians. But when finally they stood for battle at Borodino, his tactics were not of the type that had gained him the victory at Austerlitz and Jena. Nor was the battle followed up by a swift pursuit of the exhausted enemy, who was allowed to retire on Moscow, and pass through that capital without molestation and place himself in an advantageous position to threaten the extended line of communications.

The character of the Russian Tzar and the resistance offered by his people deceived the expectations of the invader, who remained in Moscow vainly hoping for the opening of negotiations which could not be expected in view of the strategic situation of the opposing forces.

When the retreat from Moscow was undertaken, the project of retiring by the Kaluga road was not pushed through with the Emperor's customary resolution; a week was thus lost and the selection of the eventual line of retreat to Smolensk led the army through an already exhausted country.

The retirement of Schwarzenberg towards Warsaw instead of Minsk exposed the flank of the retreating army. When retreat had been decided upon a concentration of all troops, including those of Macdonald and Schwarzenberg, towards the Berezina should have been arranged for. As it was, the separate parts of the army were all exposed to defeat in detail.

Many writers have tried to ascribe the failure of

Napoleon entirely to bad fortune, and have belittled the operations of the Russians to the extent of denying that they had any influence whatever on the destruction of the Grand Army. As Jomini says, to such writers " only the manna of the desert and the waves of the Red Sea were wanting to make the God of battles work miracles in favour of his enemies." But to belittle his enemies is not the way to exalt the genius of the great captain. Nor is such a course just in this instance. The Grand Army was opposed by brave troops under able and devoted leaders.

In this campaign the genius of Napoleon is no less in evidence than in his previous undertakings, although we may see faulty execution in the details of the operations. There was no blind plunge into the depths of a half-barbarous and inhospitable country. But the vastness of the distances, of his masses of troops, of his preparations rendered the task impossible of human attainment. In their conception and initiation the grandeur of his projects is comparable with his most successful undertakings.

Nor were the operations of the Russians in their wider aspects wanting in skill both in conception and execution. Their initial dispositions as well as their retirement on divergent lines were faulty, but the concentration at Smolensk of their separated wings was a masterly movement. Their avoidance of battle until the invaders had been reduced in strength by the length of their march may be commended, as well as the change in the direction of retreat after the fall of Moscow. Wittgenstein exhibited all the qualities of a great commander, and contributed largely to the destruction of the enemy by the manner in which, with inferior forces, he maintained himself on the Dwina and kept the left wing of the French engaged throughout the campaign.

In following up the retreating enemy, Kutuzov no doubt failed in resolution, in energy and in the adoption of a strong offensive. But it was a fine combination which brought about the general Russian concentration on the line of retreat from Moscow, and of large Russian forces on the decisive point and at the decisive moment at the passage of the Berezina. Had it not been for failure in execution on the part of Chichagov, the French must have been totally destroyed by that great strategic movement.

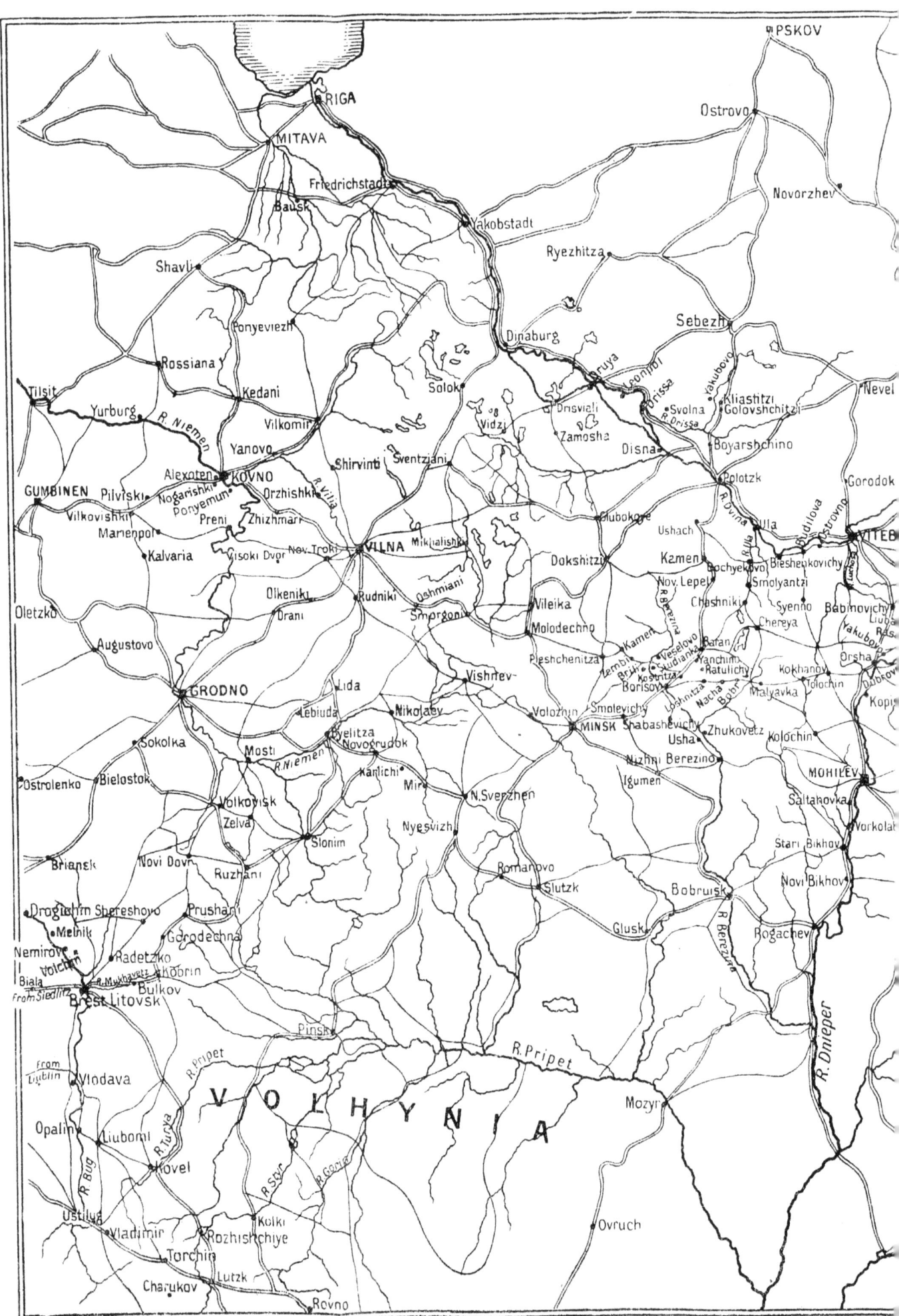

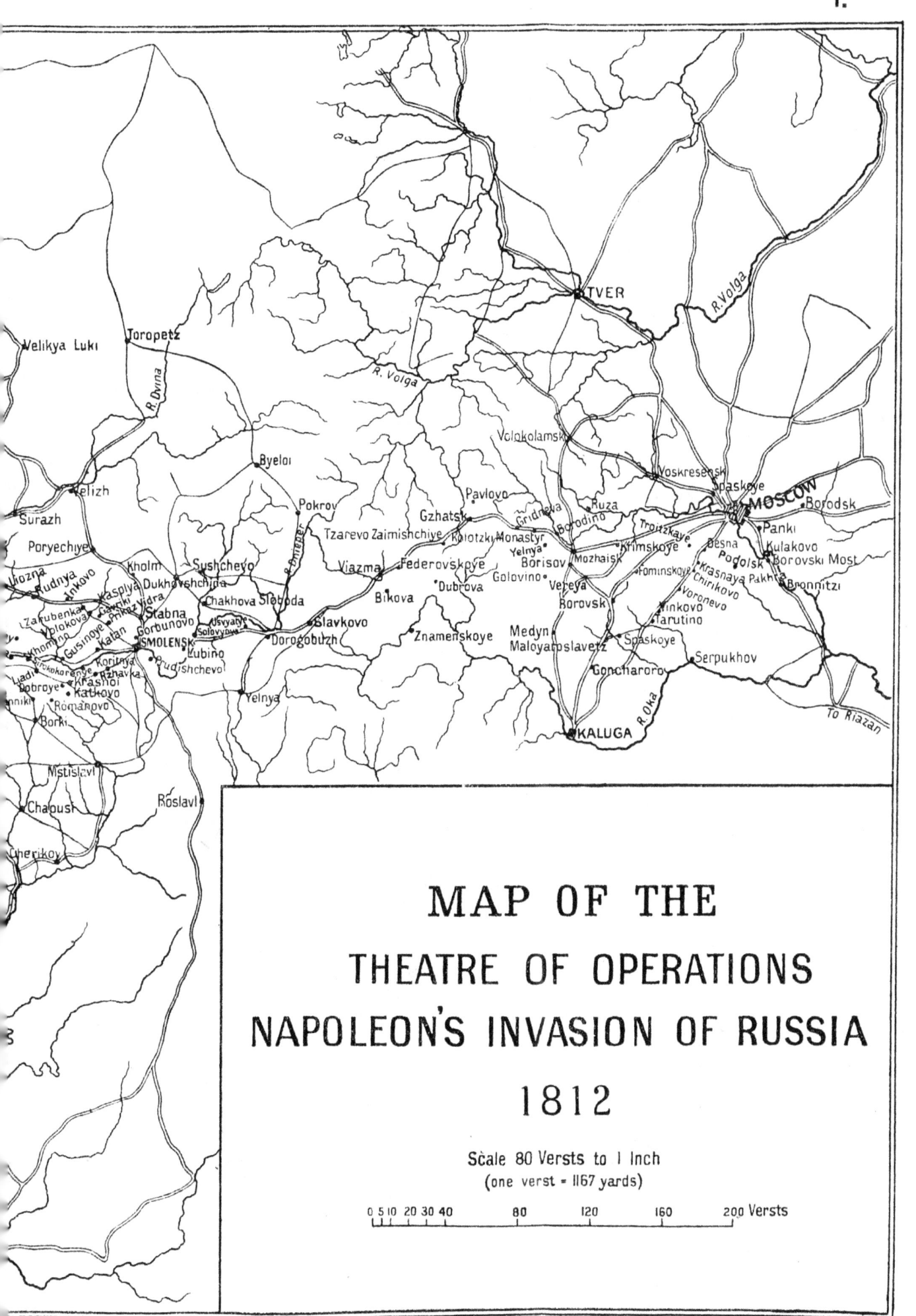

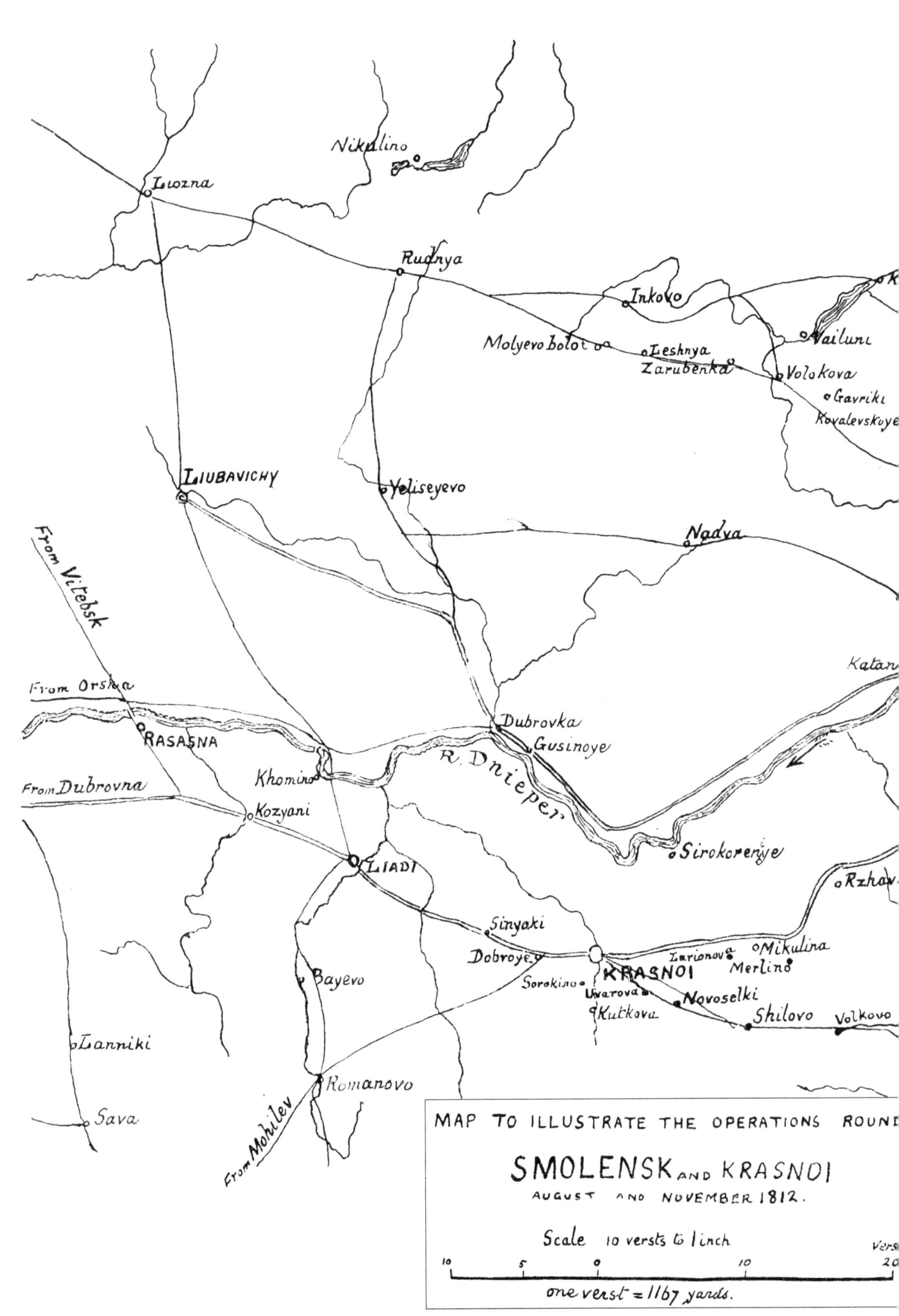

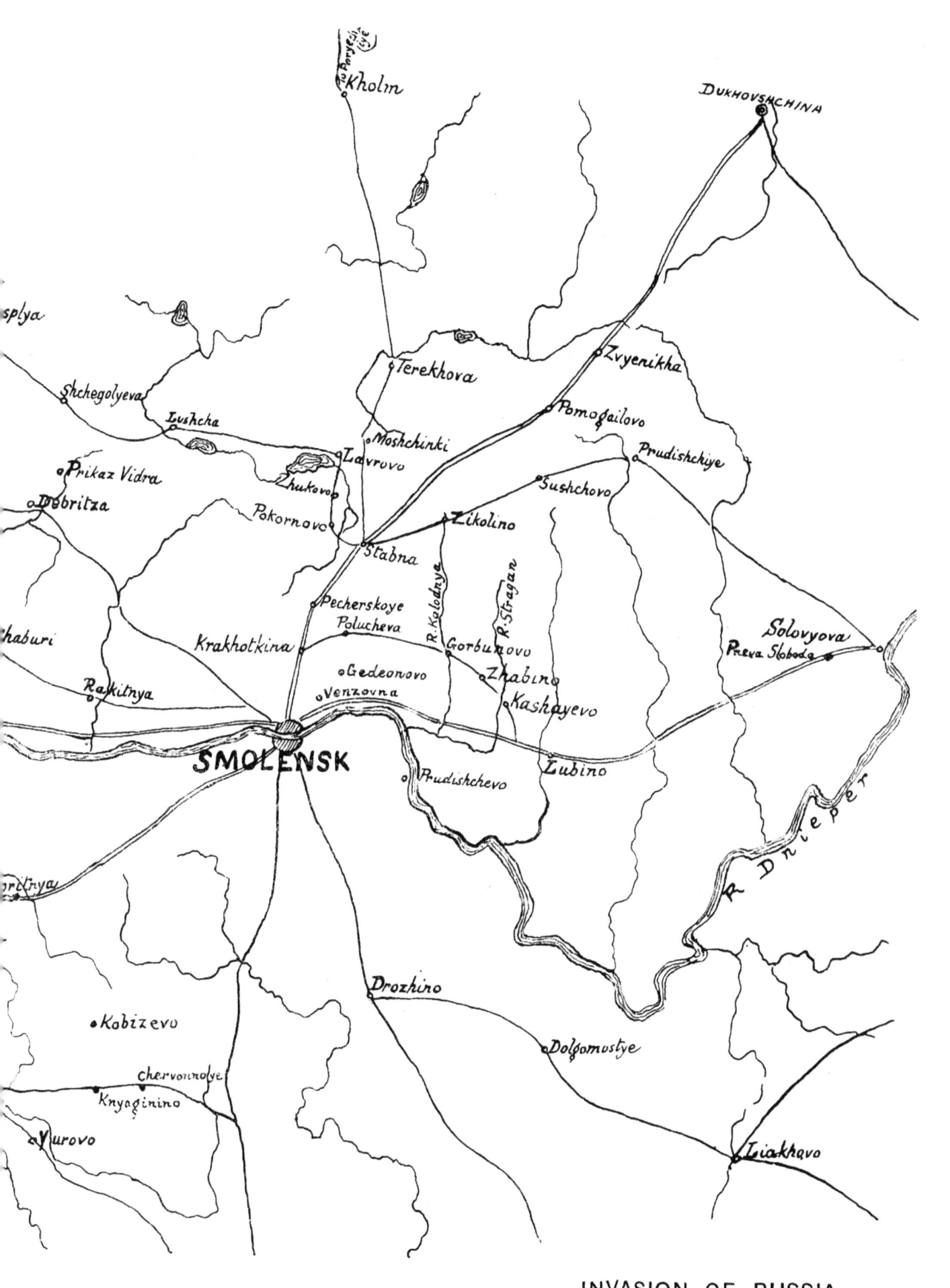

INVASION OF RUSSIA.

INVASION OF RUSSIA.

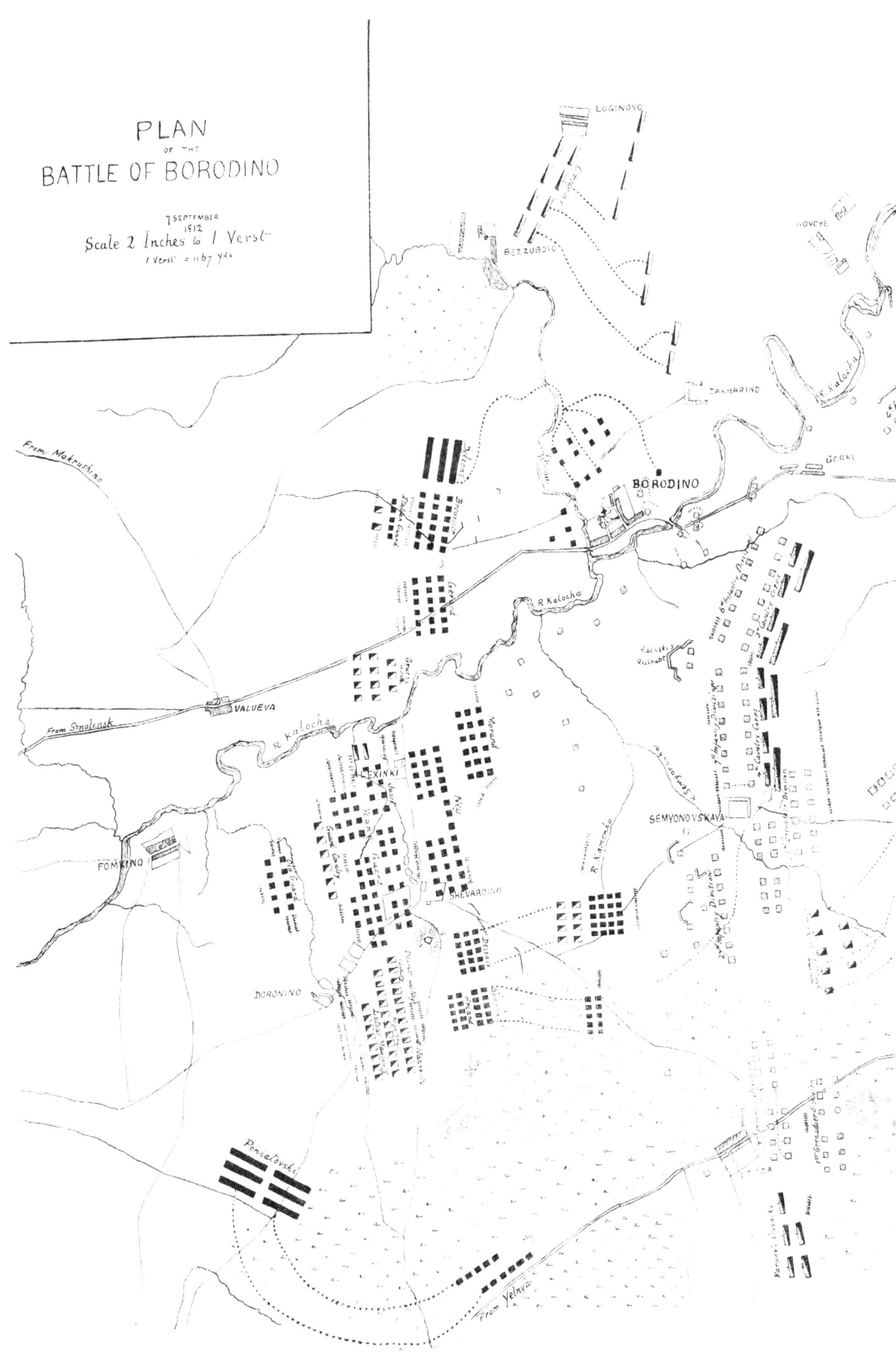

INVASION OF RUSSIA.

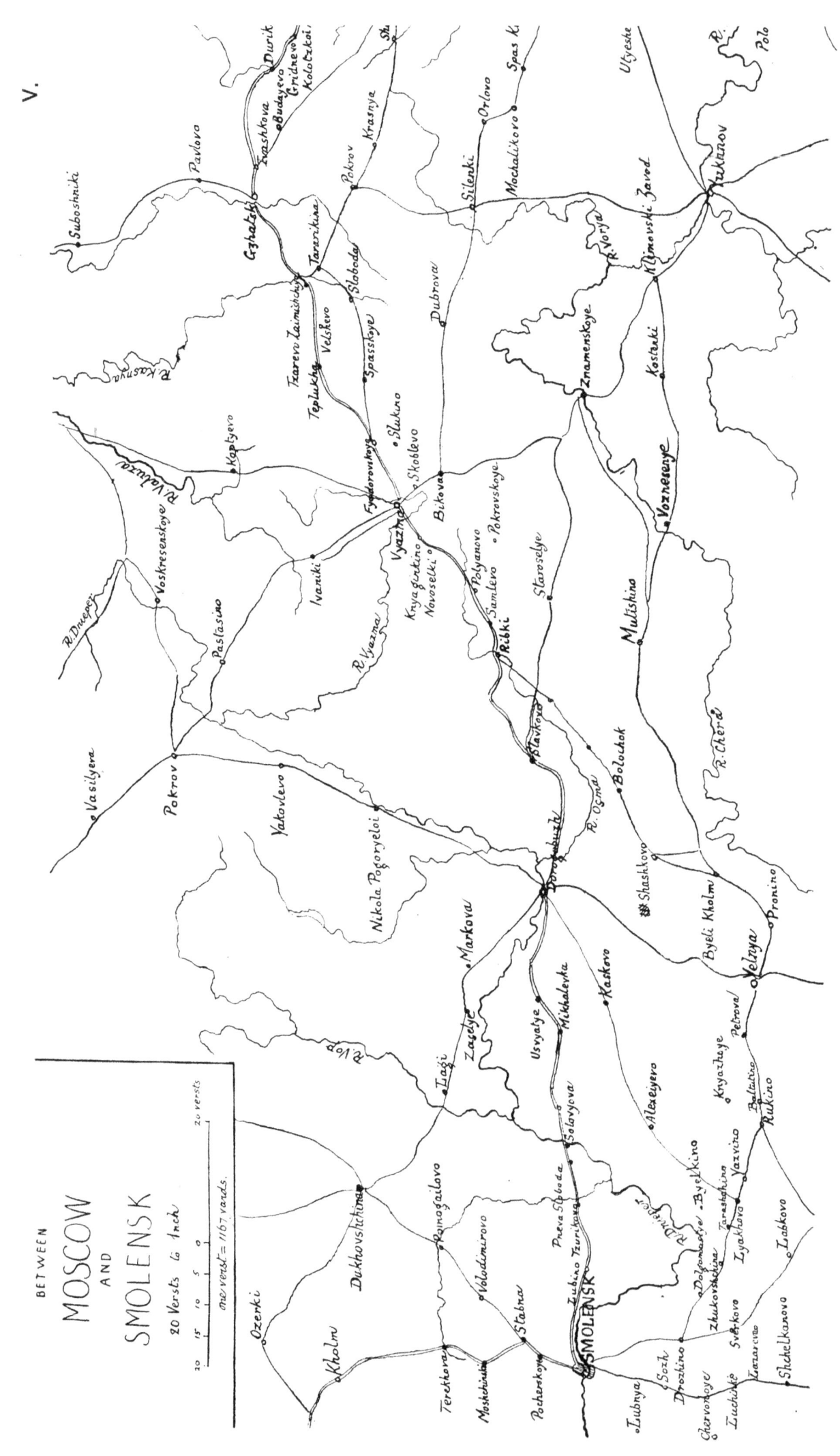

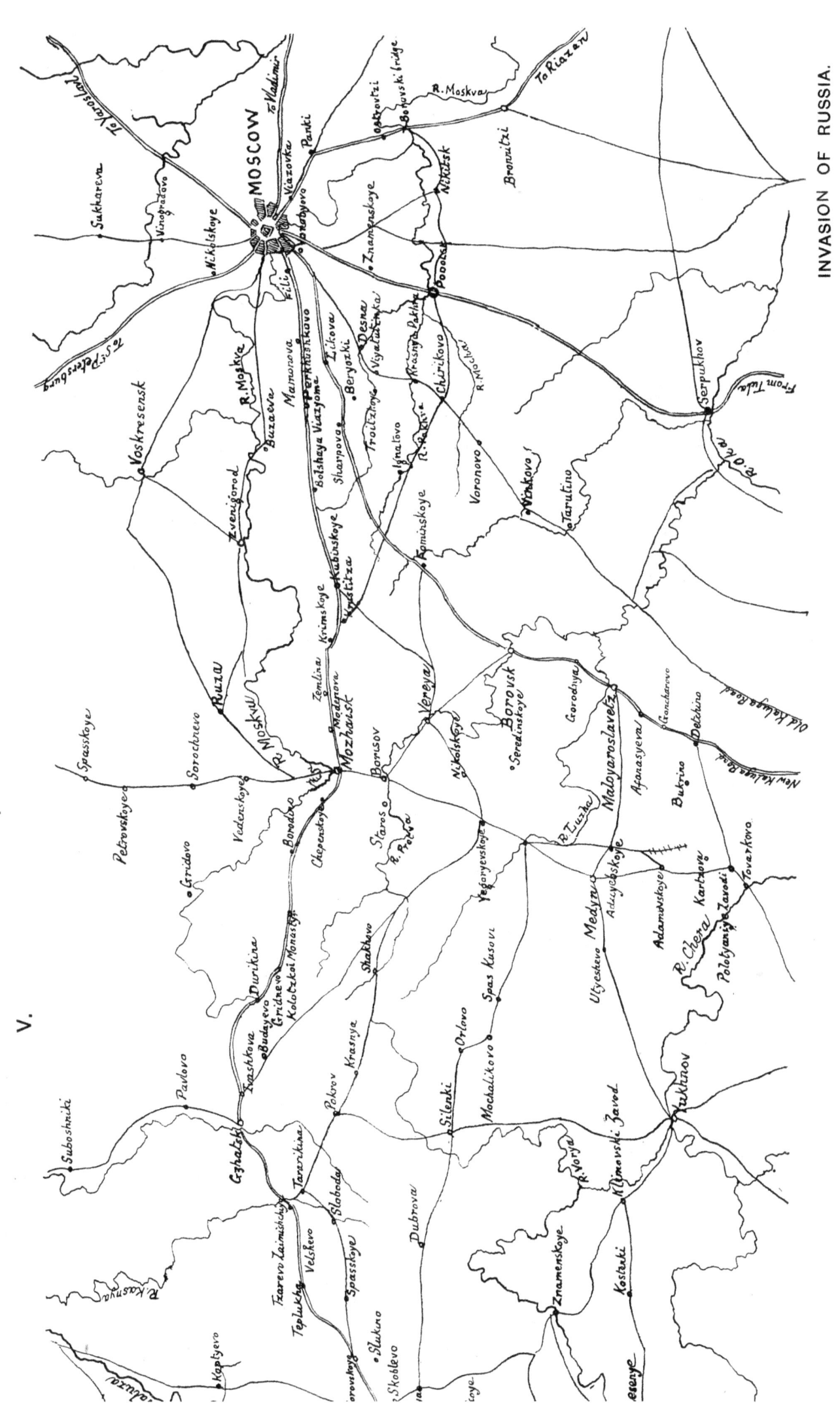

THE PASSAGE OF THE BEREZINA.

INVASION OF RUSSIA.

VI.

www.ingramcontent.com/pod-product-compliance
Lightning Source LLC
Chambersburg PA
CBHW081519160426
43193CB00015B/2731